GW01454403

# A week in

# Bigfoot Territory

By Melissa George

© Melissa George 2020

All rights reserved. No part of this publication may be reproduced, distributed, or transmitted in any form or by any means, including photocopying, copying, downloading, uploading, recording, or other electronic or mechanical methods, without the prior written permission of the publisher and/or Author.

 Although the author and publisher have made every effort to ensure that the information in this book was correct at press time. The author and publisher do not assume and, at this moment, disclaim any liability to any party for any loss, damage, or disruption caused by errors or omissions, whether such errors or omissions result from negligence, accident, or any other cause.

Cover Illustration Copyright © 2020 by Melissa George
Cover design by Melissa George
Book design and production by Melissa George
Cover Images from Morgue File, or personal images.

Names and places have been changed to protect people and properties. This story has been vetted for truth and authenticity.

Before you begin, please let me remind you that I am an Independent Author. My books are created by me. They are all written in General Casual. If you find the occasional Typo. I apologize. I don't have a group of people sitting in their office waiting to go over my book before it reaches you. The English used in the majority of my books may not be proper at times. This is better to convey the story to you just as it was told to me without sounding like a textbook, with this being said. I hope you enjoy this book cover to cover. If you do, please think about leaving me a review. Your reviews can make or break an independent author. If you didn't care for the book. I understand. We can't connect with every book. Just try to go easy on me in your review. Thank you.

**I** thumbed through my new foraging book while I sipped a cup of coffee. I didn't have but a few minutes and I was going to have to get ready for work. My book had come in the mail yesterday, but I was just too tired to look at it last night. Foraging and learning about plants was my newest thing. I could probably thank all of the survival shows I watched for this latest interest.

"Whatcha got"? Paul asked, pouring himself a cup of coffee. Paul is my husband. We have been married since we graduated from high school. That was some time ago. We are both forty-two now.

"A new foraging book," I responded, without looking up from my book. I knew I had to get up and get ready for work. However, once I got my nose into one of these books, it was hard to put it down. 'Wow! Who knew you could eat a Daylily"? I said excitedly.

Paul sat down at the kitchen table with his coffee. He was already dressed and ready to walk out the door. "Are you working today," He asked. It was more of a statement than a question. I knew he was telling me to get moving, or we were going to be late.

Paul and I worked at the local factory. It was not what we had dreamed of doing fresh out of high school.

We both wanted to go to college and move far away from small-town America. We both started working at the factory because the pay was good.

It would give us the time and the money to save up for college. Well, those savings built us a beautiful house on the outside of town. I wasn't complaining, though. It is what we both had wanted at the time, and I was happy for the most part.

As it turned out, Paul and I never had any children. We had both wanted kids, but it never happened for us. That was fine, though, we were perfectly happy with our many nieces and nephews. Plus, it gave us more time to pursue our outdoor interests. Well, it did when we weren't working. Lately, that was all either of us was doing.

I let out a sigh and got up from the table. It was going to be another long day. I slid my book toward Paul before leaving the room. I knew he would look through it while he waited on me to get ready.

The sun was starting to come up when Paul and I walked out to the car.

There was still a slight chill in the air, but the weather was getting warmer.

We were in late spring now, and summer was just around the corner. Days like this made it hard to go into work. The cloudless sky promised a beautiful afternoon, but I wouldn't get to see any of it.

We didn't clock out until four, and by then, the afternoon was already gone. I tried not to think about this too much. It would only depress me and make the workday seem even longer.

"Looks like it's going to be another gorgeous one," Paul said, looking up at the porcelain blue sky.

"I know," I mumbled. "I would much rather be up in the mountains," I added.

Paul and I had a few spots up in the mountains that were far away from the standard camping areas. We had to hike in to get to them, but that was the beauty of it to us. We loved being away from the crowds. While most people planned their vacations and headed to a beach or a hotel, Paul and I packed up our backpacks and headed up into the mountains. We fished, hiked, and just hung out by the river. That was vacationing to us.

"We could play hooky and go fishing," I suggested. Knowing that Paul wouldn't go for it. He was a supervisor now, and they had been training some new people for a few weeks.

"I'm going to ignore that you even said that," He responded. Paul preferred fishing over-breathing. I was hoping that my little poke might persuade him. We could get away with it from time to time.

We were both close to everyone in the office because we had worked there for so long.

Occasionally one of us could grab a day or two off here and there. However, with Paul training, I knew that wasn't going to be anytime soon. I resigned myself to work and got into the car. I couldn't help allowing a lingering sigh to pass my lips.

Paul heard my sigh and looked over at me, "I've got a touch of cabin fever myself," he said. "Maybe next month, I can get us a day or two off."

That would be great," I told him. It wasn't his fault that I was in this mood. I got like this every time a new book came, and I couldn't get outside and enjoy it. I didn't realize another sigh had escaped my lips.

I watched the trees go by as we drove down our small country road. Paul and I lived out of town away from everyone. We had always enjoyed our privacy, so of course, we would build a house out of town. My parents had asked us why we wanted to live out in the middle of nowhere. To us, it was still too close to civilization.

For the past couple of years, I had been trying to get Paul into homesteading. It was my dream for us to be self-sufficient.

Well, it was my dream every time I watched a TV show about it or watched a YouTube video. Other than that, I don't guess I put a lot of thought into it.

I had tried at one point to get Paul into hunting. That was an epic fail. Paul isn't big on killing animals. Then I got the idea of introducing him to Bow-hunting. I figured that would be less messy or bloody than a gun. I thought that was going to work out until I realized that he just liked shooting the bow. He still didn't like the thought of killing animals. That put a big kink in my homesteading dreams. However, I couldn't blame all the failures on Paul. I did not know a thing about canning, and I was scared to death of a pressure cooker. I had spent some time watching videos on how to do all of this stuff. Once I found out that I could blow the house up with a pressure cooker, I kind of lost interest. I started thinking that maybe we should supplement our grocery buying with a garden and some fruit trees. The garden worked great until Paul stopped watering it, and I stopped weeding it. We didn't have the time to take care of it properly. Well, that isn't actually true.

By the time we got home from work, neither of us wanted to go work in the garden. Besides, we were both working long hours, so we had plenty of money to buy all the food we needed.

Therefore, my latest interest was foraging. I had yet to eat anything I found. (I'm not stupid.)

Just knowing I could recognize the plants made me feel good. Who knows. Paul and I may find ourselves lost in the wilderness one day. He could fish for us, and I could gather plants. Besides, I had even learned about some medicinal plants. If I got good enough, I could save us a ton of money that way, Right.

The car stopped, and I was thrust back into reality. We were in the employee parking lot at Thomas Textiles. The sun was now casting short shadows across the parked cars. Seeing this depressed me even more. I grabbed my lunch bag and got out of the car. It felt ten degrees warmer than it had when we left the house. Why couldn't it have been raining today?

Paul came around the car and kissed me. We headed for the big steel doors together.

I cleaned the kitchen after dinner and flopped down on the couch, staring up at the ceiling. Paul was watching TV.

I needed to get into the shower, but I liked the idea of soaking in a hot tub a little better. My feet were killing me, and I was exhausted. I knew better than to get into a hot tub when I was feeling like this. Many people had drowned that way.

You fall asleep, and your head slips under the water. I would go get my shower just as soon as I rested here a moment.

A commercial came on TV, and Paul muted it with the remote control.

It annoyed me when he did this, but I tried not to say anything. I felt stupid, staring at a quiet screen while a girl is arguing with her husband about auto insurance.

"There's something I think I should tell you," Paul said. While Looking over at me.

He had my undivided attention. I sat up on the couch. This sounded serious.

"I was talking to Howard today," Paul started. Howard was one of the supervisors down at the plant. He had been there as far back as I could remember. He was a nice family man. He loved showing pictures of his grandkids.

It wasn't unusual for Paul and Howard to be talking, especially while training new people.

However, why did Paul feel the need to tell me about it? It looks like that shower was going to wait a bit longer.

"We were talking about all of the long hours we had put in training the new people. Howard told me that the bosses were about to make some significant changes.

Since they have hired so many new people, they are going to phase out saving up sick days. There will not be any more saved sick days after the first of the year. You will still get sick days, but if you don't use them, you lose them, along with the fact that they will only be given with a Doctor's statement.

Hearing this infuriated me! After all of the years we had put in at this plant, I felt that Paul and I deserved better! "Do we still get our week vacation, or have they shortened that too"? I asked sarcastically.

"We still get a week vacation," He responded. "But only the people that have been there five-plus years will get a paid vacation.

"What in the world is making them do all of this"? I asked.

"I don't know," Paul replied. "But that is why I went ahead and put in for our vacation and sick days."

"What"? I asked. This wasn't like Paul. He would usually talk to me about something like this first.

"I know I didn't talk to you," Paul continued as if reading my mind. "But I found out that Brett's old hunting cabin is available. And I thought you might like to spend some time up there."

"Wait. What?" I responded. A million things were going through my mind. We had time off. Brett's cabin? Where was Brett's cabin, and what did it look like? When were we going? Why did Paul get us time off?

"I know it's sudden and unexpected," Paul said. "But things just seemed to fall into place.

Brett had told me earlier that his cabin would be empty for the next few months, at least until deer season started. Then, when I talked to Howard, it gave me the idea. Therefore, I went and talked to Marshall, and he was all good about us taking some time off. I figured now would be the best time for us to go before it gets hot".

This was a lot to take in all at one time. "Where is Brett's Hunting Cabin"? I asked. I had a million questions, but it was the first one that came to mind.

"It's up in Bluestone Valley," Paul replied. "Roughly about five hours from here," he added.

"That is some pretty remote wilderness," I said worriedly. Do you think we can handle it?"

Paul smiled, "I'm sure we can. And remote is exactly what both of us need right now."

"Tell me more about this cabin," I said. "I'm not sure I want to stay in a place that I have never seen before.

And with it being a man's hunting cabin, I must say, I'm a bit worried".

Paul laughed at this. "I knew you were going to say that, so I had Brett send me some pictures." He picked his cell phone up from the end table while I walked over and sat down on the arm of his chair.

I have to admit that the first picture impressed me. It showed a small, two-story, rustic cabin set back in the woods. It had a small front porch with two rocking chairs. You could see the distant mountains over the top of the cabin. The next picture showed the back of the cabin and the back yard. The back had a more substantial porch with a swing on it, and the river was only a hundred yards from the back of the house. There was a small fire pit and picnic table. The next picture shocked me. It showed the main floor. It was an open floor plan with a kitchen bar separating the two rooms. It looked to be very clean. The living room had two beautiful leather couches and a recliner. The kitchen was small but efficient. There were a small bathroom and washroom downstairs. The upstairs had two bedrooms and a bathroom.

Both bedrooms had queen-sized beds and looked to be clean. I was shocked and very excited.

"I can't believe how nice it is," I stated.

Paul laughed aloud. "I think that might have something to do with Brett's wife," He said. "They spend family time up there as well."

Now that made more sense to me. I could not picture a man's hunting cabin being this nice.

"So, when do we go"? I asked. Now that I had seen the cabin, I was looking forward to it.

"I thought we could leave first thing Saturday morning," Paul said. "That will give us a couple of evenings to get our stuff together. And we can go Friday after work to get some groceries to take."

"Saturday?" That was quick, I thought. Would that give us enough time to get everything ready? I was looking forward to a vacation, but I was not looking forward to the work that went with it.

"Alright," I said. I was resigning myself to the fact that the next two evenings, I would be working my butt off to get things together.

"How long will we be staying?" I asked.

"Three weeks," Paul replied, while still looking at the TV. I used our sick days and our weeks' vacation. But we don't have to stay the whole time if you don't like it."

'WOW!' I exclaimed. "Three weeks sounds heavenly."

Paul gave me a huge smile.

After my shower, I headed back out to the kitchen to make lists of the things we would need to take.

At least we wouldn't have to hike into our camping area this time. Not that I minded, sometimes it was a lot of fun. Still, it was also a lot of work.

By Saturday morning, Paul and I had most of the things packed into my SUV. All we liked was grabbing a few things out of the freezer and stopping for ice on the way out of town.

I made us coffee, knowing we would stop somewhere later in the morning to eat.

Paul walked into the kitchen just as I was pouring the coffee into the cups. He looked as tired as I did. We had worked hard the last couple of days trying to get everything ready. We hadn't even started our trip, and I was already exhausted.

The morning was beautiful; it was slightly warmer than it had been, with a cloudless sky. I was feeling thankful that I was going to be able to enjoy this day from sun up to sundown.

The ride up the mountain was gorgeous. I always loved the mountains at this time of year. Everything had just turned green with the promise of the coming summer. The weather was beautiful. It wasn't too hot.

The nights were seasonally cold, and the bugs weren't flying around yet. It was just perfect for spending some time outdoors.

Paul stopped at a gas station about halfway up the mountain. I wanted to add more ice to the cooler, and Paul wanted to top off the gas tank.

Once inside, I grabbed a few snacks and headed for the counter. I would pay for them along with our ice and gas. The cashier must have seen our loaded down SUV. He asked where we were headed as he rang up my purchase.

"Up to Bluestone Valley," I said, digging the cash out of my wallet.

"Oh," he responded. "You're heading up to Bigfoot country."

"What?" I asked, looking up at him. I knew he had to be teasing me.

"Bigfoot country," he repeated. "People have been spotting them up there for years."

 I was shocked to see that he seemed rather serious.

"Really?" I asked. I was more than a little curious now.

The cashier had taken my money and was counting out my change. "Oh, yes, ma'am," he said. "People have been seeing them and hearing them all over the place up there. Some of them tell me about it when they stop here.

 I told them that they could keep that thing to themselves. I don't want any part of a big hairy monster.

"What do they tell you?" I asked. This would make an excellent story to tell Paul.

"Mostly, I get stories about them yelling and throwing rocks at people. A few have spotted them. Most everyone that talks about them tell about the size of the things. They say they are huge. Some of the foot casts I have seen make me glad that I live down here and not on up the mountain".

"Foot casts?" I questioned.

"Yes, Ma'am," says the cashier. "Some people make casts of those creatures' footprints. I have seen some twenty inches long and ten inches wide. "As I said, it makes me glad I live down here," he replied.

I picked up the brown bag from the counter.

"You guys be careful up there," The cashier called as I headed for the door. "There's not much phone signal up there. Make sure you have a satellite signal and some bear spray". I stopped in my tracks and turned back around to face him. "You said a satellite signal?" I questioned."Yes, ma'am," he said. "They help your cell phone get a signal when there isn't one," he stated.

"I don't suppose you carry them?" I asked. I already knew the answer. A very smart cashier had just suckered me.

"Yes, ma'am," He said. Nodding toward some cards on display there on the counter. I grabbed two and slid them over to him. He smiled and rang them up for me. "Sixty-nine ninety-nine!" I exclaimed. "Those are a bit expensive, aren't they?"

"Not if they can save a life." He said with a smile.

I reluctantly paid for the cards and thanked him.

Paul was finished with the gas and the cooler when I came out of the store.

"I wondered if you were kidnapped," he said with a laugh.

I didn't tell him about what the cashier told me, or what I paid for the stupid satellite cards.

Paul turned the radio on to some country station as we pulled out onto the highway. I settled back into my seat content with watching the beautiful countryside.

I thought about what the cashier had said. I guess it could be possible to have a Bigfoot out there.

These mountains did look desolate. I noticed that the traffic on the road was getting to be less and less.

Of course, I had heard of Bigfoot. The big half man-half ape that lived out in the pacific north-west. There were books and movies made about this elusive creature. I am not sure how much of it, I believed.

I guess I thought of it like aliens and paranormal encounters, anything was possible. I really did not believe Bigfoot was going to be much of a problem on this trip. We were far from the Pacific Northwest. Even though I think it would be cool to see one. Well, on second thought, maybe not. Not if they are as big as people say they are. That would probably scare me to death. As we climbed up the curvy mountain roads, I let my mind wander to what a Bigfoot would be doing in these mountains. Where would he live? What would he eat? Did he hide from people, or did he like to scare them? I was so lost in my thoughts that I didn't hear Paul.

"You getting hungry yet?" Paul asked.

"Hey." "Earth to Candi," Paul said with a laugh.

I reached over and turned the radio down. "I'm sorry," I said. "I didn't hear you."

"You must have been a million miles away," Paul said with a smile. "I was just asking you if you were hungry yet."

The small snacks we had eaten earlier had worn off, and I was getting a little hungry. "I guess so," I responded.

"Brett told me about a dinner that's just up the road. He said they had the best home cooking around. Want to try it out?" He asked.

"Sounds good to me," I said. "As long as I'm not the one doing the cooking, I'm up for anything."

Paul laughed.

Roughly, about twenty miles on up the mountain, Paul pulled into a gravel parking lot with a small building. It didn't look to be big enough to be a restaurant. Paul drove up to the front and stopped. The sign on the front said, "Bigfoot Bobs Dinner." "The finest country cooking in Bluestone."

Suddenly I felt uneasy.

"Let's go see what Bigfoot Bob has to offer," Paul said, getting out of the car.

As it turned out, the food was delicious, and the staff was very accommodating.

I can see why Brett would recommend this place. Paul and I ended up ordering dessert to take up to the cabin with us. We figured it would go good with a cup of coffee tonight.

Our waiter refilled our cups while we waited on dessert. "Where are you guys from?"

She asked, "I haven't seen you in here before." Paul told her where we were from and where we were going. The waiter smiled sweetly. "Are you two Bigfoot Hunters?" she asked.

"Well, no," Paul replied. He was giving her a puzzled look.

"Oh!" "I just assumed," she said almost apologetically. Most new people up this way are usually looking for Bigfoot." She added.

Paul laughed. "Do you think that's something we should be looking for?" he asked.

"People around these parts would say yes," She commented. "Most of the locals have seen one or knows somebody who has."

"Really?" asked Paul. I could see that she had captured his interest. I couldn't tell if he was sarcastic or serious.

What was with all of this Bigfoot talk lately? It was as if we had traveled into another dimension.

I was starting to worry just a little bit. Was there anything to these claims? Or were all of the locals a bit off? Either way, I thought it was cause for alarm. Maybe we should forget about this and go home.

"So, what exactly should we keep an eye out for?" Paul asked with a smile.

Now I could tell that he wasn't serious. Good idea, I thought — no sense in upsetting the locals.

The waiter let out a little laugh. "I'm not a Bigfoot hunter either," she said.

"But I've heard people talk about the yells and screams they do at night. They say it is unlike anything you have heard before.

And sometimes when you're out in the woods, they may throw rocks and sticks at you". She added.

"Well, we will definitely be watching and listening for anything out of the ordinary," Paul told her. "And who knows, maybe when we're back this way, we might just have a story for you."

"I will be looking forward to it," she said with a smile. "Now, let me get those desserts for you."

Back in the car, Paul said, "Now what did you make of that?"

"Well, I responded, "Normally, I would have brushed it off. But after talking with the man at the gas station, I'm starting to worry about the locals", I told him with a little laugh.

It didn't take long for me to tell Paul about the conversation at the gas station. I left out the part about the satellite cards for now.

I was feeling a little embarrassed about that. I felt like I had fallen for a scam.

"I wonder why Brett has never said anything about this," Paul replied. "You would think that he would have mentioned something."

I did not respond as we turned off the main road onto a gravel driveway.

The driveway didn't look like it was used in ages. The grass had grown tall in the center, and in some areas, it looked like it had almost been washed away. The trees barely gave enough opening for a car to get by. I wondered why Brett hadn't fixed this.

After bumping along for what seemed like forever, I finally asked Paul, "Are you sure this is the right road?"

"Brett told me that it was off the beaten path," Paul said. "And it would seem like a pretty good drive-in.

But once we reached his road, there was no way we could miss it."

"Well, that's good to know," I said sarcastically. There is no way we could turn around, even if we wanted to. I could hear our stuff shifting around in the back, and I was hoping it wasn't much further.

"We should be there soon," Paul said. Reaching over and patting my leg.

The road curved back and forth while it steadily climbed up a steady incline.

Just as I was about to give up all hope, we rounded a corner and was in front of the cabin. It was so sudden that Paul had to hit the brakes, causing us to slide a little on the loose gravel.

"See. I told you," Paul said with a big smile.

I got out of the car laughing at the way we had arrived. It was nice to be out of the car. The fresh mountain air smelled terrific.

I looked over at the cabin. The two rockers were missing from the porch, and the wood looked a little more weathered than the pictures showed. Overall, it looked like it would be an excellent play to stay.

Paul must have seen the uncertainty in my eyes. "Shall we go have a look?" he asked.

He walked around the car, taking my arm, we walked toward the front porch together. You could tell that no one had been here in quite a while. Leaves were blanketing the front porch. They had to have been here since last fall. Didn't he rent this place out? I thought. Surely, someone would have cleaned up.

Paul walked over to the edge of the porch and picked up a rock from the ground. There was a small hole beneath the rock.

Paul put his hand down into the hole and pulled out a shiny key, returning the rock to the top of the hole. This impressed me. That was a pretty cool way to hide a key.

The steps creaked as Paul and I walked up onto the porch. The dry leaves crunched under our feet. This was the moment I had been waiting for. Paul put the key into the lock and gave it a turn.

With a slight push, the front door swung open. We were hit with the musty smell of a cabin that had been closed up to long.

My eyes were slowly adjusting to the dim room. At first glance, it didn't look too bad. I stood there as Paul fumbled around for a light switch. The lights came on, revealing a living room with the two leather couches we had seen in the picture.

By the look of the sofas, I assumed the photo was taken years ago. At least everything seemed to be clean.

Paul walked over to the far wall and drew back the floor-length curtains. The view of the mountains was breathtaking! "Oh my!" I exclaimed, walking over to the windows with Paul. "This view is gorgeous."

"I don't think I could ever tire of seeing this," Paul stated, looking out over the mountains.

Leaving Paul to admire the view, I went to see what was available in the kitchen.

The kitchen was small, with a single bar separating it from the living room. The bar had two stools on each side. With the limited space, I was sure this was used in place of a table and chairs. In the kitchen were a stove, refrigerator, microwave, and a coffee pot. It had all of the necessities. I was pleased with this.

Just off the kitchen were a small bath and a laundry room. It looked like it had been a laundry room to start with, and the bathroom was added as an afterthought.

Paul joined me to check upstairs. We found the staircase just inside a small narrow door on the far side of the living room. The staircase was very narrow and dark.

We slowly navigated the steep steps and came out on a small landing with a door on each side.

The bedrooms were very similar, both with a queen-sized bed and a small dresser. The bathroom was in the center connecting the two rooms. I was satisfied that it looked clean enough. Yet I did want to get some windows open before we unpacked.

While Paul and I walked around opening the windows, we noticed that the ones on the backside of the house had been nailed shut. This did not make a bit of sense to either of us.

We just assumed that Brett might have had a problem with vandals and left it at that.

After we got our things brought into the house, we decided to see the river.

The back yard was very overgrown. The grass and weeds were knee-high, and some small trees looked like they were about to take over. Why had Brett let it get this bad?

There was a small shed to the left of the yard. I wondered if the lawnmower was kept in there. As if reading my mind, Paul said, "Brett told me there were some tools in the shed if I needed to clear a path." This answered my question. Brett did know that his property was this bad. Why would he let it go like this?

I followed Paul as we made our way through the tall grass down to the river.

The river itself was about twenty feet wide at the edge of the yard. It was pretty calm here, but you could see that it was rushing a little faster once it passed the property and made its way down to the first bend. I had to admit that it really was gorgeous.

"Would you look at that," Paul exclaimed excitedly. Upon closer inspection, I could see the brown trout swimming around the rocks in the river. I knew right then that I would be unpacking most of our things myself.

That was just fine with me. It was the whole reason we came on this trip in the first place. To relax and enjoy ourselves.

"You got get your fishing gear, and I will get started on the unpacking," I told him with a smile.

"I know I'm going to owe you big," he said as we started back toward the house.

"Just get us enough fish for dinner, and we'll call it even," I responded.

Two hours later, I opened the patio doors and stepped out onto the back porch. I had the kitchen arranged as I wanted it, I had made our bed, and I had our suitcases in the bedroom.

I had placed our hiking gear in the adjoining room out of the way. Now, with a fresh cup of coffee in my hand, I was ready to sit down for a few minutes. I could see Paul on the river from where I sat. I would go down and get him once I got dinner started. For now, I was just going to sit here and enjoy the view of the mountains.

As I sat there sipping my coffee, I thought about getting outside tomorrow and seeing what type of plants I could identify. I was excited about it. I had even put a new app on my phone that was supposed to help. I was just sitting there looking out over the forest and thinking when I saw something black move in between the trees.

At first, it was so sudden that I couldn't be sure if I had seen anything at all. However, after staring in the same location for just another minute, I saw the black movement again.

From where I sat, I couldn't make out what it was. I stood up to get a better look. Black bear scared the daylights out of me, but this thing seemed too big to be a bear. Black bears did not usually get very large.

I knew Paul would be well equipped with bear spray and a gun. It was just the fact that one could be so close scared me to death.

As I stood up, Paul looked across the river in the same direction as the black thing I saw.

I wondered if he had heard or seen it. My heart was racing. Did I run to grab my bear spray and try to make it down there? Did I yell for Paul?

I didn't know what to do. I stood there, holding my breath to see what was going to happen. I glanced at Paul and then back up into the trees. Where did it go? I couldn't see it now. There was no way anything could have gotten gone that fast. I stood there looking all through the surrounding trees, but now there was nothing there at all. Could it have just been a trick of the light? Well, it really didn't matter either way now. Paul was getting his stuff together to come up to the cabin.

We were sitting on the back porch that night when I told Paul about what I had seen through the trees. For a split second, I thought I saw the look of alarm on his face, but it was gone as suddenly as it came. "Was it a black bear?" I asked.

"I didn't see anything," Paul responded. I honestly wasn't sure if I believed him. I thought he was trying to keep from scaring me. He knew how I felt about the bears.

"Well, I saw something," I told him. "And it wasn't far from where you were fishing."

"Well, we knew there might be bears," Paul said. "We will just be cautious and we'll be fine," he assured me.

I looked out into the dark night. I knew what I had seen was not a bear. It had been too tall to be a bear.

Well yes, I know that a bear can stand up on its hind legs. This thing had seemed to be walking upright between the trees. Bears did not cover any kind of distance walking upright.

For the first time, my mind went to the Bigfoot everyone had been talking about today. Was it possible? Could something like that exist out here in the mountains? I guess logically it could. There was plenty of food, water, and places to hide. This was the first time I had ever considered the possibility of Bigfoot being real.

I knew I had seen something out there today. I also knew that it wasn't a black bear.

I was pondering these things when Paul got up from his chair.

He said, "Don't get yourself all worked up over nothing." He patted my shoulder as he walked by. "I'm going in to see if this TV works."

I sat out on the porch a little longer. The night air was beginning to get chilly. I scolded myself for overthinking what had happened earlier.

It could have been a trick of the light, and here I was jumping to conclusions. I had to stop this, or I would be too scared to go foraging tomorrow. I got up and went inside.

Paul was looking at the vast array of movies on the bookshelf. He had never been a movie kind of person, so this was interesting. He thumbed through the videos mumbling about there not being any satellite. I guess we were out in the boondocks if there was no satellite. Paul usually watched Documentaries and things on the travel channel. To get him to sit and watch a movie with me was next door to impossible.

"Well, what looks good"? I asked. Sitting down on the couch.

"Our choices are pretty slim," he responded.

I knew that with Paul, it probably would not matter what the movie was about, he wasn't going to like it.

"What are you in the mood for"? He asked. "Comedy, Drama, Action, Documentary or Thriller"?

I thought I would be nice and choose Documentary.

Paul put the disk in the player and went to pour himself another cup of coffee. I got comfortable on the couch as the opening credits played. I was shocked to see the words Bigfoot dance across the screen.

I wasn't sure how I felt about this. Part of me wanted to learn more about these creatures. Yet a part of me was terrified by the thought that these monsters could actually exist.

"Are you trying to scare me?" I asked as Paul sat down on the opposite couch.

"I just thought this might be interesting since we are supposed to be in the middle of Bigfoot country," he replied, with his eyes glued to the screen.

I had to admit that it had me a little intrigued too. By the time the show went off, I was on a roller coaster of emotions. I was fascinated. I wanted to know more.

Yet I was also scared to death that these things were actually out there. They were huge! Luckily, they seemed to think that they are more curious and elusive than aggressive. Still, the thought of coming across one in the woods was frightening.

The show also showed us some things that they think these creatures create in the woods. They are called stick structures. They just looked like mini Teepees to me. I could see how something like this would look out of place in the middle of the woods.

'Well, what did you think"? Paul asked. Getting up to stop the player.

"I hope they stay on the other side of the mountain," I said with a smile.

Paul let out a laugh before taking our coffee cups out to the kitchen.

I hadn't been trying to be funny. I did not want to run into this thing at all.

That night my dreams were full of large hairy creatures roaming the woods.

The next morning showed signs of being a beautiful day. The sky was blue without a cloud in sight.

Over breakfast, Paul and I discussed what we wanted to do for the day.

We knew that we would be here for a whole week, at least. This gave Paul plenty of time to enjoy fishing from the river. Therefore, we decided to take a hike today and do a little exploring.

After I cleaned the kitchen, Paul and I packed our small shoulder bags for a day trip. We would plan a camping trip once we had gotten to know the land a little better.

Just as I shouldered my pack, I realized that I had left our phones on the charger in the bedroom. I went to get them and slid the two cards I had purchased into my back pocket. It wouldn't hurt to have them just in case I thought.

I had utterly forgotten to see if we had phone service here! I quickly turned on my phone and waited for the bars to appear- Nothing. I walked closer to the window and tried again—still nothing.

Now, this was frustrating. I had wanted to use my new app today. I grabbed one of my books with a notebook and pen. These would have to do if I didn't have cell service.

The sun felt amazingly warm as we walked down across the back yard. I was thoroughly enjoying this.

I breathed in deeply of the fresh mountain air. This was going to be the best few weeks ever.

Walking along the edge of the river was peaceful. The birds were calling overhead.

A squirrel would bark at us from time to time, and occasionally to Pauls' delight, a brown trout would slap its tail on the water. Paul and I lived for these days. Being out in nature and far away from the everyday hustle.

As we walked, I pulled my phone out of my back pocket. I still didn't have a signal. I held it up in the air, hoping to catch a spot that would connect. Absolutely nothing.

Paul glanced over his shoulder and saw me waving my phone around like a flag.

"I forgot to tell you that there isn't a signal out here," He said. I stopped in my tracks. Looking at him as if he had just turned green. "And just when were you planning on telling me this"? I asked.

Paul stopped walking and turned to look at me. He let out a sigh before he started talking, letting me know that he had been avoiding this for as long as possible.

"There are no signals out here, Candi. The towers can't get signals because of the mountains". He said. "That is why there is no TV or power either." He added. The signals just cannot get past the mountains.

'Wait", 'What," I asked. "How is there no power when the stove and coffee pot worked fine this morning, not to mention the hot showers we had," I added.

"Brett has a generator that runs on oil and gas. He told me how to fill it if I need to," Paul added.

I was just about to ask another question when Paul began to talk again. He had been married to me long enough to know what my next question was going to be. "The nearest hospital is close to fifty miles away. However, there is no need for you to start worrying now. We're going to be fine." He said. "And besides, Brett said that he would drive up from time to time to check on us." I just stood there with my mouth hanging open.

I loved the outdoors, but I also wasn't stupid about it either. Not that we had ever needed it, but it was just safe to have police, fire, and rescue just a phone call away.

I wasn't sure how I felt about being out here in this remote wilderness with no one to help if a bear attacked us, or we fell and were injured, got sick, and a million other problems that had just popped into my head. The cards! I reached into my back pocket and pulled out the cards I had bought at the gas station.

I handed them over to Paul with a triumphant smile. Paul carefully examined them, then asked, "Where did you get these"? "At the gas station," I told him with a smile. I was feeling good about myself.

Paul let out a sigh handing the cards back to me. I was perplexed. "These would be perfect if we had satellite phones." He told me. "I'm not even going to ask you what you paid for those." He said with a smile.

Satellite phones? Well crap. Maybe I should have looked the cards over before I paid for them. I had just assumed that these would be what we needed.

Knowing now that they were useless really put a damper on my morning.

I didn't even know there was a difference in our phones and a satellite phone, and I wasn't about to ask Paul.

He would happily explain it to me, but I would end up looking stupid in the process.

"Come on," Paul said with a smile. "We're going to be fine."

Let's go find us a nice spot to camp for a day or two." Paul continued up the river. I reluctantly followed mentally kicking myself for being so gullible.

It didn't take long before I forgot about the phones and was once again enjoying our walk. I could tell that by the way, everything was grown up that no one had been on this river in a while. Definitely not this year. With the weather starting to get warmer, that may change.

However, it was secluded now, and that was all that mattered. If I remembered correctly, Paul said that Brett hadn't rented the cabin out in a few years.

If that were the case, we wouldn't have to worry about seeing anyone the whole time we were up here. Other than not having my cell phone, this was pure heaven.

I was wholly absorbed in my thoughts when Paul came to a sudden stop in front of me. "What"? I asked. Wondering what had made him stop.

"I thought I heard something growl," He replied. Looking across the river.

"What did it sound like"? I asked.

"It wasn't a bear," Paul said. As if to calm my worries.

The river was moving slower here, making it easier to hear, yet I didn't hear anything.

We stood silent for a few moments with both of us listening. Then I heard it. It was more of a low tone howl than a growl.

Paul turned to look at me with his finger over his lips, indicating that I should be quiet. Of course, I was going to be quiet. I wanted to know what was making this noise as much as he did, and he was right, it was not a bear. While we stood there listening, I heard something that sounded similar to a woodpecker, but it only knocked one time. Paul looked at me, raising his eyebrows as if to say, "That sounded strange."

I was just about to open my mouth to whisper to him when a tree fell pretty close to us.

It was so loud and unexpected that it caused my heart to leap up into my throat. Bringing with it a surge of adrenalin.

"Holy Crap!" Paul exclaimed.

"That sounded pretty close," I thought aloud.

"Let's go check it out," Paul added.

I wasn't sure why Paul wanted to go see a fallen tree. What else did we have to do out here? I figured we might as well.

We hadn't walked far at all when we found the downed tree.

It was actually just over a slight hill from where we had been standing. It was easy to see that this tree was a Big-tooth Aspen. These trees grow to be huge and don't usually fall so easily.

This one looked to have been alive and well before it fell over. This thought struck me as odd. I didn't know of any bug or fungus that could cause this to happen, and their roots were usually pretty deep and solid. I guess there were a million reasons a tree could fall in a forest.

Paul walked all around the tree, examining it from every angle. I stood there and watched, wondering what he was doing. Finally, he looks up at me and asks if I notice anything odd.

"Well, yes," I tell him. "This tree seemed to be alive up until the time it fell over," I stated.

"You're right," Paul replied. "And there are a couple of other things that don't add up. The tree looks to have been healthy.

It doesn't have any rub or claw marks on it that I can see. The roots appear to be intact, and it fell up-hill. This tree seems to have been pushed over", He stated.

"What in the world could push over a large, healthy tree"? I asked. I felt like we were possibly overthinking this whole fallen tree.

Paul straightened up and raised his eyebrows at me.

"What"? I asked. "What did I say"? I didn't understand why he was giving me such a strange look.

"There is only one thing, other than a tractor, that could push this tree over."

"We would have heard a tractor," I stated.

"Exactly," Paul said with a smile.

"I don't get it," I stated.

"We learned a little about it on TV last night," Paul replied.

It took me a minute to grasp what he was saying. When I did, my heart flew up in my throat, and my adrenalin kicked in.

"You don't mean a bigfoot"? I questioned.

"That is precisely what I mean," Paul replied. "It is the only explanation that makes any sense."

I didn't even want to consider it. From what we had watched last night, I knew he was right in thinking this way, but there had to be another logical explanation. There was just no way any of those creatures could be in these mountains. It was not possible. Someone had to be out here messing with us. That's what it was! Someone knew we would be here, so they were out here in the woods playing a joke on us. I looked around quickly but didn't see anything.

"Have you considered the fact that someone could be out here playing a joke on us"? I asked Paul.

The look Paul gave me let me know that I had just said something that was well beyond stupid.

"What in the world makes you think that someone would be out here in the middle of nowhere pushing over trees just to try to scare us"? He asked.

"If anyone overheard Brett and me talking, they are more than likely working their shift at the plant right now.

And besides, did you see anyone leaving the area?" '

He questioned with his arms held out to show the vast area of the woods.

As much as I did not like to admit it, he was right. I knew with everything in me that he was right.

There was a good chance that one of those creatures was right here in the woods with us. Just allowing myself to consider this possibility scared me. I was just about to tell Paul that I thought he was right, but the yell that came next stopped my words along with my thoughts. It was unlike anything I had ever heard before. I had spent years in the woods. I thought I had heard all of the animals that were out there. This didn't seem to be purely an animal. It had an element of human mixed in.

Something about it that made my blood run cold and piqued my interest at the same time: I still found myself scrambling forward to get closer to Paul.

We were both looking at the distant ridge, the area the yell seemed to have come from. "Amazing," was the only thing Paul said. He had a look of fascination on his face.

I knew right then that Paul was going to want to know as much as he could about what had just made this noise. I did too.

Paul and I looked around a little more, but we didn't venture out too far.

After hearing the yell, we knew that we weren't alone, and we thought it might be best not to aggravate anything.

We looked at the surrounding area carefully and then decided to head back to the cabin. Neither of us wanted to come face to face with this thing just yet. We had a lot more to learn. We had found a smaller version of a stick structure, but we didn't see anything else.

Paul spent the afternoon fishing while I foraged for plants. I came across a few that I had to look up, being that I was out of our general range. But I noticed that there was something odd. There was an overabundance of Broadleaf Plantain here. It seemed that the majority of it had been dug up. This was odd to me because most animals won't eat it. This plant is well known for its medicinal properties, and I always looked for it when we were out camping or hiking. It could come in handy for a few different things. It was good for insect bites and itching, and it could be used as an anti-inflammatory. The whole plant could be consumed safely.

I had only used it for insect bites and rashes. Why was so much of it missing?

As I paid more attention to the plants that were missing instead of what I could find. I started to see a pattern forming. Along with the Plantain, there was a lot of yellow root missing. I also saw some peppermint that was not indigenous to this area.

I didn't think Brett's wife had planted any because what I was finding was random.

These were medicinal plants that covered a whole range of ailments. With these three things, you were pretty much covered. Pain reliever, anti-inflammatory, upset stomach, insect bites, rashes, antibiotic, sore throat, stuffy nose. Just about everything you could think of. I knew these particular plants wouldn't be missing unless someone knew exactly what they were used for. Did the Bigfoot know this? Were they using these plants? I wanted to look this up online, but we had no internet out here. This was frustrating. I walked down to the river to talk to Paul.

Paul and I decided that when we went into town for supplies that we would look for the local library. We could access their computers to do a little research.

That night after dinner, we found more Bigfoot documentaries. When I say "more," I actually mean that we found a lot. It seems that Brett or someone in his hunting parties had a fascination with the creature. That was fine with us. Paul and I both had become interested in learning more about them.

We watched two shows that night that were in much more detail than the first one. I was thankful for this.

I learned that most people that had encounters with them said they felt no need to fear for their lives. The Bigfoot had shown no sign of aggression; they appeared to want to be left alone.

Now this changed my whole outlook on being out in the woods. I no longer feared that I would be somethings dinner.

Before going to bed that night, Paul and I talked about how excited we were to check out the woods again. We were both feeling better now that we knew there was nothing to fear.

The next morning was overcast and looked like it was going to rain at any minute. Paul and I were anxious to get back out in the woods and decided to take our chances. I packed us each a Poncho in our day bags. At least if it did begin to rain before we got back, we wouldn't be completely soaked.

Paul and I started walking up the side of the river. It didn't seem to take as long to find the spot we were at yesterday when we heard the first yell. We both stood still and listened. The woods seemed to be eerily quiet today.

Just as Paul and I were about to start walking again, I heard something.

I reached out and grabbed Paul's arm, signaling him to stop. Our footsteps were making a lot of noise on the dry leaves, and that is what I was hearing. Something was walking through the leaves!

I estimated the sound to be roughly thirty yards away. (I'm not good at judging that sort of thing.) We couldn't see what it was due to the trees and underbrush. I knew it was on the same side of the river that we were. The river was to our right, and this noise was coming from our left. Paul took my hand, and we slowly began to walk at an angle from the sound. This should put us directly in its path if it continued to walk a straight line. My heart was beginning to race. Now all of a sudden, I was getting pretty scared. What if this thing got angry because we were out in the woods? We were encroaching on its territory. It could easily decide that it didn't want us there. I tried to think of the things they said on the show last night. They weren't out to kill us.

This thing could be hunting or merely trying to get from point A. to point B.

By the time Paul and I made it to the top of the ridge, there was nothing to see. The footsteps had plainly come in this direction. I had been hearing them just until the few seconds before we topped the ridge.

"How did it just disappear like that"? Paul asked. Was it standing still now listening to us?

We stood there for just a moment listening. A light rain had started. I felt the first cold drops hit my face. Before we could decide to stay or go, the rain quickly got harder. We were going to be drenched!

Then we heard it, it was so close to us that the sudden noise scared me. "Whooooop!"

This sounded like it was just beyond the trees directly in front of us! I would guess that it was only ten or fifteen feet away.

"Holy Cow!" Paul exclaimed as he pointed in the direction the sound had come from. "It was just right there"! My adrenaline had kicked in again.
"Whoooooop!" This one came from behind us! This one sounded like it was just a few feet down the river! The rain had become so fast that it was getting hard for me to see. The water was running down us in rivers.

We hadn't had time to get our ponchos on, and we were completely soaked.

With the second call, Paul got a slight look of concern on his face. "I think we had better head back," he said, taking my hand.

"What's wrong?" I asked, slightly louder to be heard over the heavy rain. If we were in any kind of danger, I wanted to know.

Paul leaned in closer to me so that he wouldn't have to yell over the torrential rain. "I don't like feeling that we're being surrounded." He said. " This is their territory, and we need to leave."

The wind was beginning to pick up now, and the walk home was going to be difficult at best.

With the weather being so bad, we almost passed the trail going up to the cabin! Just the thought of what could have happened had we missed that trail scared me to death. I think it bothered Paul as well. He commented that on the next sunny day, he would get that trail widened.

After we both had a hot shower and now with a steaming cup of coffee in hand, we sat down at the bar.

I had gotten out my notebook so we could write down the things that we wanted to look up online.

We both seemed to have many thoughts and ideas about this. This hiking adventure sure had taken a turn. I would have never in a million years thought that Paul and I would have a fascination with Bigfoot. Yet here we sat, both of us entirely consumed on learning more about these creatures.

The rain continued all afternoon heavily. Luckily, Paul and I both packed books just for days like this. I cooked a big pot of chili to have throughout the evening.

We both spent the afternoon curled up on the couches. This is where I would usually catch up on my reading. Today it was all about the documentaries.

We watched hours of Bigfoot documentaries with me jotting down notes here and there.

Just before dark, I went to the kitchen to put on another pot of coffee. The rain had begun to let up, but it was still falling steadily. I assumed it would rain most of the night. I was hoping it would be bright and sunny tomorrow.

I had my back to the windows that faced the river as I filled the coffee decanter. I heard what sounded to be a small rock hit the glass, I stood there a minute listening and a second one hit. I thought about the landscape outside.

There weren't any trees close that would be dropping anything onto the cabin,

especially at this time of year. The sound was so faint that it was barely audible. I walked over to the window just as another one hit the glass. It was harder, this time. Paul heard it too because he turned the volume down on the TV and walked over to where I was. When the next one hit, it scared me. Each one seemed to be a little harder than the last. I actually heard this one land on the porch.

"Who would be throwing rocks at the cabin"? I asked Paul worriedly.

"I don't know," Paul replied. "Probably just some kids." He walked over and flung the door open. "You better stop that!" He yelled out into the darkness.

Who did he think he was yelling at? We were in the middle of nowhere. I think Paul realized this after he closed the door back. He looked at me with a puzzled look. As if he were confused. For a split second, sheer panic consumed me. Was Paul having a stroke or heart attack? How would I get help?

"I guess that didn't do any good," he said with a sheepish grin.

"Probably not," I agreed with a slight chuckle.

We had to run off some neighborhood kids a couple of times at home.

I guess they didn't think anyone lived there since we were so far out. I am sure now this is what Paul had been thinking.

By the time I poured our coffee, I had realized the rocks had stopped hitting the window. Could it have been kids? I just didn't see how or why kids would be out here during a downpour. Maybe Paul and I could look around tomorrow to see if there were any houses closer than we thought.

Paul put another movie on, and the rocks were soon forgotten. I didn't think about them again until I saw them on the porch the next morning.

I couldn't help myself, but my thoughts went to the Bigfoot in the area. Would they do something like this, and if so, why?

I called Paul over to show him the small rocks that were lying just below the kitchen windows. "Who do you think did this"? I asked.

Looking down at the small rocks, Paul replied. "Who or what." I was hoping he could give me a logical explanation, even though I knew there wasn't one.

"Do you think there are any families that live around here"? I asked. Hoping that maybe there were.

"I don't think so," Paul responded. "Brett told me that our nearest neighbors were roughly fifteen miles away. And that's if you go across the top of that mountain", he said, pointing to one of the more massive mountain ridges. "Those people are seasonal too. So I wouldn't expect anyone to be over there at this time of year". He added.

"Well, now that we have ruled out people, what's left? I wondered. This thought both excited me and scared me...

Paul and I had decided that we would leave out early, spending most of the day in the woods. We wanted to look for more evidence, but we also wanted to find a good spot to camp for a few days.

We headed out that morning with our day packs a little fuller than usual. I had packed us each a few bottles of water along with more snacks than we would normally carry.

We walked off the porch just as the sun was peeking over the mountain ridge. The sky held a few high clouds that were catching the sun with magnificent color. It held the promise of a beautiful day.

The air was still a little chilly, but it would be warming up soon enough. I felt good and was excited to spend a day in the woods.

Paul wanted to head up the river first as we usually did, but also spend some time exploring the lower part as well. We hadn't been down the river yet, and we were both curious to see if it held as much evidence as the upper part.

The walk was nice, and before we stopped for our first break, I knew we had to be a couple of miles in. We had come across some small stick structures earlier. Which I promptly took pictures of. Paul and I were keeping records now on our findings.

We would note the day and time, the general area, and then take pictures. Paul said this could show us if there were any patterns. It made sense to me.

We stopped at a beautiful area up on a ridge. We were both a little tired. I sat down with my shoulder bag and began digging inside it. I was starving from all the walking we had done, and I thought that a granola bar with an apple would be good right now. Paul had almost finished one bottle of water and was digging inside his own pack.

The ridge gave a nice view of the mountains ahead of us, but the trees blocked the view below.

That would be the direction we would be going next, and it looked a little steep to me.

"Do you think we'll have any problem going down"? I asked Paul.

"Not with going down," Paul answered. "But maybe with stopping," he said with a smile.

This was typical of Paul to make a joke when he knew I was concerned.

"I think we will go down this ridge and then follow the valley floor back down the river," Paul though out loud. "The walking will be easier once we reach the ravine."

I hoped he was right. I was tired and didn't know how much more of these mountains my legs could take. Maybe this break would help.

I was right. The cliff was steep here, and we had to use the trees to ease our way down. It didn't take long for my legs to get shaky and my arms to start burning. Paul was trying to be as encouraging as he could by saying things like, "not much further now." And, "We've got this." By the time we made it to the bottom, I had to sit down again. Paul leaned against a tree to catch his breath. That had been a lot harder than I had imagined.

I looked around as I sat there resting.

The ravine was flat, and about thirty yards across where it cut between the mountains. It was pretty here. The trees were sparse, creating an opening in the center of the ravine. The water from the river formed a small creek that ran right down the middle.

I thought that it would be a beautiful place to camp. I was just about to tell Paul when he doused my thoughts.

" This would be a great place to spend a night or two if it wasn't for these mountains," Paul said, looking up at where we had just come from.

"What do you mean"? I asked.

"Well, normally, this wouldn't bother me, and the mountains would shield us from any bad weather. But now with this being possible Bigfoot country, I don't want us boxed in down here". He added.

I hadn't considered the fact that we may need to get out in a hurry. I hadn't even thought that we may need to run. Well, this put a whole new spin on things. I was grateful that Paul was watching out for us.

Just as I was about to stand up, Paul quickly reached out and grabbed my arm. He pointed to something across the ravine. I couldn't see anything at first, but then I saw something brown moving through the trees.

It was moving slow, and I couldn't make out what it was. I stood up to get a better view. We both stood quietly with our eyes fixed to the spot. Both of us were unknowingly holding our breath. Whatever this was, moved on up the ravine away from us. It didn't seem to be bothered by the fact that we were there, or hadn't even noticed.

Finally, about forty yards away from us, it walked out into the open. It was just a deer—a beautiful buck with a huge rack. I felt my whole body relax. The buck suddenly raised its head as if it heard something and bounded off back into the woods.

I was just about to tell Paul that it must have smelled us when I saw something out of the corner of my eye that made my blood run cold.

To our right, not even ten feet away, was a bear! What was strange was it appeared that the bear was sleeping with its back to us. I quickly put my hand over my mouth to stifle any noise I might make. A wave of fear shot straight through me! Paul and I could be in the fight of our lives at any second!

Paul must have seen the bear about the same time that I did. He squeezed my arm and leaned in close to whisper, "Don't make a sound. Slowly, head for the tree line over there".

I was terrified that I would make a noise to give us away.

My worst fear was being lived right now, and my mind didn't know how to handle it. Luckily, my feet began to move toward the tree line on their own. I was taking extra care with each foot placement. The slightest noise could give us away.

It seemed to take forever for us to make it to the trees. Once I made it to the edge of the ravine, Paul took my elbow and whispered, "Just a little further." We moved on into the trees a little. I turned around then and looked back at the bear. It didn't seem to have moved at all. Something didn't feel right. I was thankful that the bear hadn't spotted us before we could put some distance between it and ourselves. I still felt that something wasn't right about this.

"I don't get it," whispered Paul. "How did it not hear or smell us"?

I told him that I had been thinking the same thing.

We stood there for a moment looking at the bear, and then Paul whispered, "Come on." He motioned for me to follow him. He pulled the bear spray out of his pack and handed it to me as he unholstered his gun. I didn't like the way this seemed to be going. I did not want to be any closer to that bear than we already were.

I knew I wasn't going to leave Paul to face this by himself, so I reluctantly began to follow him. We walked up the side of the ravine until we could see the bear from another angel.

"It looks dead," Paul said. "I know how strange that sounds, but it looks dead," he added.

"I think it's just sleeping," I said worriedly.

"Well, there is only one way to find out," Paul said. "Get ready."

My heart began to race, and my stomach tightened up. I knew we were about to be fighting this bear!

"HEY BEAR"! Paul yelled. His voice cut through the ravine like a gunshot, causing my heart to beat even faster with the sudden noise.

I was starting to feel light-headed. I kept telling myself that this couldn't be happening.

To our amazement, the bear didn't move!

Paul then bent down and picked up a river rock about the size of his hand. I wondered if he would be able to throw it that far. He answered my question when he gives it a hefty lunge. I couldn't believe that the rock bounced right off of the bear, and the bear never moved!

"That answers our question," Paul said.

I was shocked! Why hadn't the bear moved? Was it playing with us?

"Come on," Paul said. Taking my hand.

He was going to walk over to the bear now.

Everything in me screamed, no. Something didn't feel right.

Before I could explain my feelings, I was crossing the ravine floor with Paul pulling me along. As we slowly approached this bear, I was beginning to see why it hadn't moved. The bear looked to be dead. When we got up next to it, Paul took his foot and forcefully shoved it over. They were no marks on it. No gunshots, no signs of it being in a fight. The only thing was the neck. The neck was broken. How in the world had this happened?

I immediately looked up the mountain to see if it could have fallen. There was no way.

The trees would have broken its fall, and we should be able to see a few broken limbs. There was nothing.

Paul was bending over examining the bear closely. "I don't understand this at all." He said. "This bear didn't just show up here with a broken neck, something had to do this." He straightened up and looked around the forest.

"I know what you're thinking," I told him. I was beginning to think the same thing.

"I just don't have any other explanation," Paul responded. In that few seconds of silence just after Paul spoke. I heard a whistle come from the trees. It was close to the area that we had seen the buck earlier.

This whistle sounded man-made. Paul's head whipped around to look.

There had to be someone out here with us. Paul put his finger to his lips, signaling me not to talk. Then he motioned for me to follow him. We moved slowly to where this whistle had come from. Maybe we could find out who it is. As we got to the area, we still hadn't seen anyone, so Paul called out "Hello"! We waited for a response- nothing. Paul called a few more times, but it proved to be useless. Either there was no one out here or they weren't going to answer us. After a while, Paul and I continued with our hike. We did get some pictures of the bear, just to document it.

Seeing that bear had made me uncomfortable. Paul and I had no clue what these Bigfoot creatures were capable of. Sure, we had watched some documentaries, but there was still a lot that we didn't know. I was starting to second-guess our efforts.

We walked through the ravine and came out on the river. We made our way downstream, paying close attention to our surroundings. Both of us were a little jumpy after seeing the bear.

We found even more stick structures and a couple of Xs. There were a whole lot of arches. Paul and I had stopped by the river for him to get a closer look at one of these arches. The tree was about eight inches in circumference.

The top of the tree was pulled down with a large rock holding it in place. The stone was on top of the branches to hold the tree down in a bent shape. Paul and I had seen these with dead logs holding them down as well as the rocks. We didn't understand why these were created or what they meant. It was fascinating to see them. However, each thing we found raised more questions.

Paul and I stopped for another break. We had found an area that looked like it would make a beautiful camping spot. The bank of the river was level here with a small sandbar. The trees were sparse close to the river, giving us the perfect location for our tent.

After resting for a while, Paul and I decided to head back. We had no idea how far we had walked, and we wanted to make it back to the cabin before dark.

Neither of us was familiar with these woods, so we didn't want to try to make it out after the sun went down. I had asked Paul just how much property Brett had here. I found out that he owned two hundred acres, and that two hundred acres backed right up to a national forest. We would have no shortage of places to camp or hike. I wondered how someone could afford two hundred acres. That had to have cost a small fortune.

Paul informed me that the property was handed down for a few generations in Brett's family, so it actually didn't cost him anything.

I had just stood up and slung my pack over my shoulder when something hit me in the back. It wasn't hard enough to hurt, but it sure got my attention. I spun around to see what it was. There was a small river rock lying on the ground. Was I just hit by a rock? Paul must have seen my puzzled look.

"What is it"? He asked. Lifting up his own shoulder-pack.

"Something hit me," I responded.

"What"? Paul asked. In disbelief.

"Something hit me in the back just as I stood up," I told him. I bent down and picked up the rock. "This is the only thing I see."

Of course, Paul reminded me that we did watch something about this on TV.

I had already thought of that before he mentioned it. I slipped the rock into my pocket, then Paul and I started our long walk back.

We had been walking for a while, and the sun was beginning to set in the western sky. It was creating the most amazing colors in the clouds; however, I was praying we would make it back to the cabin before dark.

The hike didn't take as long as I had anticipated, and we were walking across the back yard in no time.

Paul and I were talking about our upcoming camping trip when we both stopped in our tracks. Someone had just yelled "hello"! We looked up at the cabin to see Brett sitting on the back porch. I felt the relief flood over me. All of this Bigfoot stuff was starting to make me jumpy.

Brett had made a pot of coffee, and it was a welcome sight. The three of us sat on the porch and chatted before I excused myself to make dinner.

I wasn't too surprised when Paul asked him about his thoughts on Bigfoot.

Brett let out a little chuckle and said, "I see you have spoken with some of the locals."

"What"? Paul questioned. "Do you not believe them"?

"It really doesn't matter if I believe them or not," Brett stated.

"They believe it. And the majority of them claim to have seen one. That in itself is enough to make you wonder if there is anything out there".

I was unsure of how to take Brett's answer. I felt like he knew more than he was saying. But why? "Have you seen or heard anything around here"? I asked. He couldn't avoid answering my question. I just wondered if he was going to lie or tell the truth. I was starting not to like Paul's friend Brett at all.

Brett took a sip of his coffee and let out a sigh. "There is no way of getting around that question. Ok, this is just between us", he added. "A year ago, I had leased the property out to a friend with a hunting party. They were up here hunting deer. They had been here about three days when my buddy called me all freaked out. He said that someone kept throwing rocks at the cabin in the evening. Then while they were sleeping, someone would open the windows from the outside. He didn't tell anyone about this next thing but for me. He swore he saw a big hairy arm reach through the window one night and take his watch from the nightstand. I didn't know what to make of this. My friend wasn't one to make stuff up. So I drove up here, planning to spend the night with them and see what was going on.

By the time I got here, they were all packing up, getting ready to leave. My friend stayed here with me that night while the rest of them cut out of here as if their pants were on fire.

Just after sunset, sure enough, the small rocks began to hit the back windows. This went on for quite some time. I was finally fed up and walked out on the porch. I yelled out into the darkness, "You had better stop before you break my windows"! The night was eerily silent.

I turned to go back inside when I heard a scream that was so loud it actually hurt my ears. I knew that no human could make that sound. I hurried back inside and locked the door. My friend was white as a sheet.

After this, things calmed down for a little while. We turned off all of the lights as if we had gone to bed, but we were really sitting up watching the back windows. Just like he had told me, the bedroom window began to slowly open. I sat there watching this, too shocked to do anything. The window moved all the way up, and then this big hairy arm reached inside! I wanted to see what this thing was, so I quickly turned on my flashlight. The face in the window was unlike anything I had ever seen before. It was easily three times as big as ours was, and it looked like a cross between a gorilla and a man. It let out one of those blood-curdling screams and was gone".

I sat there with my mouth wide open. How was I supposed to respond to this? I had not expected this at all. Now I knew that Brett was an honest man. And I knew that Bigfoot was here without any doubt.

If they weren't still here, they had been at one time. I looked over at Paul and could tell that he was as blown away as I was.

"WOW," I said. "Thank you for telling us." This certainly explained the nailed shut windows on the backside of the house.

While I found his story fascinating: it unnerved me at the same time. I told him about the videos we had watched and the things we had found out in the woods. Now it was Brett's turn to look shocked. He said that he had never watched any of those videos. He had bought them all at a yard sale and put them here in the cabin for his renters to have something to watch. Paul told him that he really felt like something was going on here. Brett wholeheartedly agreed with him. He told us that was precisely why he didn't spend any time up here anymore.

I excused myself to cook dinner why the men chatted. I invited Brett to have dinner with us before he left. But he declined, saying that he wanted to head back down the mountain before it got too late.

Paul and I sat down at the bar to have dinner. I asked him if Brett had said anything else. I assumed that Brett would be more comfortable talking to Paul without me.

"Oh, yes," Paul said before taking a bite of his food. I waited for him to finish chewing so he could tell me. To my amazement, Paul took another bite of his food.

I wanted to know what Brett had said! I reached over, picked up Paul's plate, and sat it beside mine. This caused him to laugh. "Ok, Ok," he said. I'll tell you. Just give me my plate back". I returned his plate and waited for him to get a sip of coffee.

Paul took a deep breath and started. Brett told me that he had seen a few things himself when he first bought this place. Most of the time, he had assumed it was a bear, so he didn't think much about it.

When he finally heard what the locals were saying, he started taking a closer look at some of the strange activity around here. He was hearing yells and screams at night. Something would get into his garbage cans, but it would only take the paper plates. They would be completely gone without a trace. Then there was the time that he forgot and left a bag of apples in his truck. The next morning his truck door was open, and the apples were gone. There was mud all over the side of his truck as if a dirty bear had stood up and leaned against it. He never found any trace of these apples.

He began to notice enormous footprints on the bank of the river. One time he had left a whole stringer of fish in the water and walked up to his truck for his filet knife. When he came back, the fish was gone, and there was one wet footprint on a dry rock. It looked to be sixteen inches or better. He came up here one more time after the events with his friend.

His wife refuses to come back up here at all. That is why he is considering selling the place.

He wanted to see this thing one more time to be sure of what he had seen.

He said he felt like he couldn't think about anything else. He took a leave from work and came back up here by himself. He said nothing happened for the first few nights. But he woke up one morning just about daybreak to it raining in the back windows. All of them had been opened during the night. He walked through the house, closing the windows. When he got downstairs, the French doors were standing wide open, and big muddy footprints were leading into the kitchen. Nothing was out of place, and nothing was taken. The prints looked as if someone big had walked in, then turned and walked back out. He walked over to close the doors, and to his surprise, it was standing on the bank of the creek looking up at the house.

He walked out onto the porch in the rain and stood there looking at this thing as it stood there looking at him. He described it as being black and about nine feet tall. It was covered in hair. Its head had a small crest that started above the brow line and went across the top toward the back. Its arms were longer than ours, almost down to the knees. Its face was the same face he had seen in the window. It looked almost human.

The nose appeared broader and flatter, and the eyes more prominent. It stood there, gently swaying back and forth.

Brett said he had no idea how long they stood there watching each other. It seemed like forever to him.

Finally, this thing turned and walked into the edge of the woods. It stopped and looked back at him before it disappeared. Brett said that was enough for him. His question was answered. They existed. They were here, and that's all he had wanted to know.

He left that day and never came back. He said that he was thinking about selling the place and being done with it.

I was amazed at what Paul had just told me. I cannot even imagine waking up to find all the windows open and the muddy footprints! However, I would love to see one standing on the riverbank! I wanted that so badly.

How could Brett just walk away from this without wanting to know more? That would drive me nuts. I wanted to know everything about them.

Paul and I decided to drive into town and find the library in the morning. Along with a grocery store to buy our supplies for camping.

It wasn't hard to find the library. The town was tiny. It looked like time, and the modern world hadn't touched this place. I was utterly in love with it.

The women in the library were beneficial in showing us the computers and helping us find the best books on our subject. We didn't even get any of the strange looks I had expected.

Paul and I spent hours researching without even knowing it. I was amazed at what we found. There were tons of things online about Bigfoot. There was so much information; it made it hard to distinguish what was truth and what was made up.

How had I missed this my whole life? I mean, I knew that people claimed they existed. But I never knew it had grown to this magnitude. Paul and I both were frantically taking notes.

It was late afternoon when we finally left the library. I don't think we would have left then, but we were both starving.

We found a local diner and took our notebooks in with us. I was anxious to go over what we had found. Paul had even printed us a map of Brett's entire property.

Luckily, it was well after the lunch crowd, so the diner wasn't busy. Paul and I found a table in the back and promptly ordered cheeseburgers and fries.

By the time the waitress brought our food to us, Paul and I hardly even noticed her. We were discussing the things we had found and were oblivious to anything else.

We had the map on the table between us. We were marking where we had found different things. To my surprise, we had not come close to covering the whole property. Brett's acreage included a lot of vast wilderness. Also, it butted right up against BLM land. (The Bureau of Land Management is an agency within the United States Department of the Interior responsible for administering public lands. With oversight over 247.3 million acres, it governs one-eighth of the country's landmass.)

This would make it tricky to know precisely where Brett's property stopped, and the national forest started. It was all uninhabited. While Paul and I discussed the best way to cover this area. A man walked over to our table. He looked at me with a sweet smile and said, "If you don't mind." He reached for my pencil, which I handed over without even thinking.

He marked an area near the northwest of Brett's property. Right up near where the properties bordered.

"You don't want to miss this area," he said again with a smile. Then he turned and left the diner.

The bell on the door jingled eerily before falling silent. Paul and I just looked at each other. What did he mean by that? "We didn't want to miss this area? What was in this area? Had he overheard our Bigfoot conversation?

Just then, the waitress came over to our table. "Let me get you guys some coffee and dessert," she said sweetly.

"Coffee sounds great," I responded.

She smiled and said, "Good. And the dessert's on me". "John didn't bother you, nice people, did he"? She asked.

"John,"? I questioned.

"The man that came to your table," She responded. "That's John Baker.

He is one of the locals and a regular in here. He claims to be a Bigfoot expert. But not too many people believe what he says. John has never been quite bright, so we just humor him. He doesn't mean any harm". She said with a smile.

"Oh," I responded. "No. He was just fine," I added.

The waitress left to get our dessert and coffee.

"What do you think he meant"? I asked Paul.

"I'm not sure," Paul said. "But it wouldn't hurt to take a look at the area." Even if there is nothing there.

"We wanted to check out the whole property anyway." He added.

"I guess your right," I said thoughtfully. "It's not like we would be wasting our time by checking it out."

It was dark by the time we got our groceries and returned to the cabin. As I walked by the French doors with an arm full of bags, I stopped dead in my tracks. I could have sworn I saw a dark shadow standing on the riverbank. When I looked again, there was nothing there. I assumed I had thought of Bigfoot too much for the day. I was starting to see things.

During dinner, Paul and I picked out the area we would check out tomorrow. It was in the general direction of where we wanted to camp, just a bit further up.

It was a couple of miles short of where the man circled our calendar. They were calling for a chance of rain tomorrow, and we didn't know if we would be able to make it out that far.

Paul and I studied our notes until it got late.

Everything we had found went right along with what we had been watching on the documentaries. There were still more questions than answers. I think this is what made people want to research this creature. There was a burning need to find some sort of answer. No matter how small.

I lay in bed that night thinking about everything. The encounters Brett had sort of scared me, yet they intrigued me. Why was that? And what had the man at the Diner meant? What did the stick structures mean?

 And why were they getting so close to us without letting us see them? It was all one big puzzle, and I needed to find some answers. I fell asleep listening to the mournful cry of the coyotes and wondered if they roamed the forest with our elusive Bigfoot.

The morning was overcast and looked like it would rain at any minute. Paul and I debated whether to go hiking or head back to the library. We were both anxious to get back out in the woods, so we put on our rain gear and grabbed our daypacks.

Once we were outside, we realized that it had rained overnight. Everything was wet. This would make the walking a little slower, but neither of us wanted to postpone the hike. We had found some interesting ideas online that we wanted to try.

This time, I had a jar of peanut butter in my pack, and Paul had two bags of apples. We had read that they will take the lid off a jar of peanut butter and will take a whole bag of apples out of a tree. The apples reminded me of Brett's missing apples, so I was anxious to try it.

I was aware that it could take a few days for them to do anything, but Paul and I had time.

The wet leaves were making our footsteps quieter, but they were also slick, so we had to be more careful with placing our footing.

I'm not sure how far we had walked. Paul didn't want to get the map out and risk getting it wet. A light drizzle had started just after we made it down to the river. It was fluctuating from fine drizzle to a light mist. This was causing some fog and making it hard to see more than a few feet in front of you. I was nervous; Paul and I were not familiar with the territory. One of us could easily walk off a ridge. We did change our plans from hiking all day to leaving our stuff out for the Bigfoot and then heading back.

I had been walking with my head down to stop the rain from getting in my eyes. Just as I looked up, I saw something brown moving through the trees to our right, toward the river. I reached out and grabbed the back of Paul's shirt, stopping him immediately. Without saying a word, he turned to look at me.

I pointed in the direction I was looking. Something brown, almost red, was walking through the trees as if it didn't have a care in the world. It looked big enough to have been a bear, but bears didn't walk like this. It was walking upright. My heart skipped a beat. Was this a Bigfoot?

Were we actually watching one? With the way the trees were, we were only getting quick glimpses of the brown in between. However, it was enough to know that there was something over there walking. When Paul turned to look at me again, I could see the excitement on his face.

Whatever we had seen was gone just as suddenly as it appeared. It left me wondering what it had been.

"Come on," Paul said, grabbing me by the hand. We were now heading in the direction we had seen this thing. I wasn't at all sure this was a good idea. What if it was still there, but we just couldn't see it. I wanted to learn all I could about these creatures, but I also wanted to give them their distance. I knew that sneaking up and startling one probably wasn't in our best interest.

As we hurriedly walked toward the river, I let out two loud coughs. I was hoping that it would give whatever this was a chance to get gone. And Paul couldn't kill me for coughing. Well, I didn't think he could. His head suddenly whipped around, and he gave me a look that told me I had better die before I coughed aloud again!

Satisfied that I had made enough noise. I followed Paul
down to the riverbank.

At first, we didn't see anything out of the ordinary. Then
Paul found a few freshly broken limbs. Making it obvious
that something had been through here recently.

I walked to the edge of the river, looking across at the
other side. I couldn't help but think about Brett seeing
one standing on the riverbank. That is when I looked
down, and my breath caught in my throat. I called Paul,
but my voice came out as a small squeak.

I cleared my throat and called him again. Right beside
my boot was a massive footprint. And it was perfect!

Paul and I found more footprints, and we examined
them carefully. We measured them and took pictures. I
even recorded them on my phone. We were both upset
that we couldn't cast them because of the rain. I was
hopeful that we would find more.

Paul decided that this might be the best place to leave
our treats since we knew that something had been here.
I had to admit that it sounded like a good idea.

I looked around, wondering where I was going to leave
a jar of peanut butter. I couldn't just sit it on the
ground. Other animals could run off with it. Luckily, I
spotted a tree stump a few feet away. It was about
waist high and would be perfect for what I needed.

I unscrewed the lid and removed the paper from the top of the jar. I replace the cap, only giving it two complete turns. I didn't want it fastened all the way, yet I wanted it to be secured enough that something with hands would have to twist it to get it open. I finished with my jar and went to help Paul tie the bags of apples up into the trees. This proved to be a little trickier.

We wanted them to be high enough off the ground that other animals couldn't get to them, but we didn't have a ladder. This left poor Paul having to climb up into a tree.

 I have to admit that I laughed more than I can remember laughing in the past ten years. Paul isn't as young as he used to be, and we are both slightly overweight. This made his tree climbing skills a little precarious, to say the least. At one point, Paul was trying to pull himself up into a tree, and I was trying to push him up into it from behind. I finally had to stop and just laugh at the two of us. I bet the Bigfoot in the area now has a story to tell!

We finally got our treats placed to where we were happy with them and headed back to the cabin.

I was hoping to hear a yell or a whoop on the way back, but the rain was getting harder, and there was no sound at all except for the drops hitting the tree leaves.

The next day dawned sunny and warm. This would be the day that Paul and I could find our campsite, and hopefully, be ready to camp by tomorrow. We had our morning coffee as we packed our bags to head out for the day. We knew that our treats were probably just as we had left them, but we were both excited to go and see. We went ahead and carried more with us in case what we had left was taken during the night.

We hadn't gone far when we heard our first tree knock. Paul and I both stopped to listen. Another one, off in the distance, quickly followed it. This was great!

It let us know that they were out here and that they were watching us. I hoped our day would be full of activity. I was feeling good, so I shouted out, "Good Morning"! Paul gave me the raised eyebrow look. I figured that we didn't know how smart they were, and there is a slim possibility that they know what we are saying. So yelling out a good morning to them couldn't hurt anything.

I noticed that we both picked up our pace as we neared the spot where we had left the treats. I spotted the red lid to the peanut butter jar before we got to the area. It was on the ground and roughly twenty feet from where it should be.

Paul stopped and picked it up, giving me a wide grin. Something had gotten the lid off! We examined it carefully.

There was no sign of teeth marks on it, so another animal hadn't chewed it. The lid was intact. We could see that the jar was still sitting on the stump. A closer inspection lets us know that something had eaten most of it. There was still no bite or chew marks around the top. However, something had consumed about three-quarters of the jar! How? I couldn't think of any animal that could have done this. How could they get the peanut butter out of the jar? The opening was too narrow for something to get its head inside. Maybe an Opossum could have, but surely, it would have chewed on the plastic also. And how could an Opossum unscrew the lid? Paul had a theory that I found hard to dismiss. Something with fingers like us could have used their fingers to reach down into the jar to get the peanut butter out. Of course, we had no proof of this. It just seemed to make better sense than just a wild animal. I left the partially eaten jar on the stump, placing the lid back on it with only two twists. I left the new jar right beside it in the same fashion. It would be fun to see what happened next.

The apples in the first tree, closest to the peanut butter, were gone. There was no sign of them anywhere.

It looked like they were pulled off the rope they were tied with. There was no sign of them or the plastic bag they had been in.

Paul and I spent some time going over the area thoroughly, and there was nothing to be found. No plastic and no apple scraps. The next tree was closer to the river. These apples were still in place. It didn't look like they had been touched at all. Paul replaced the bag that was gone after more laughing from me as we tried to get him back up into the tree. I was thinking to myself that there has to be an easier way to do this.

Once we were satisfied with our gifts. We walked back down to the riverbank to scout for tracks. The ones that were there yesterday had since been washed away by the rain. And we didn't see any new ones. We slipped back into our backpacks and started on up the mountain. Paul and I were going to try to make it to the area the man had circled on our map. Both of us wondered what he had been talking about when he marked it. Then when the waitress said that he was a Bigfoot researcher, it gave us a better understanding of why he would mark an area on our map. We could only assume that this might be a good place to look around.

We stopped a few times before we got there and took pictures of tree structures. As we neared the area, I saw some things that concerned me.

We saw a couple of areas where all of the trees were pushed or blown over! It was a big area that looked like a tornado had touched down. There were just a couple of clues to let us know that it wasn't weather-related.

The first thing was that all of the trees had fallen in the same direction. I know that wouldn't be so strange with a heavy gust of wind. However, some of them had to fall uphill. Most of the trees that I have seen fall or blown over didn't go uphill.

The second thing is that there was a huge X marker made with two trees standing up directly in the middle of the ravaged area. It looked eerie placed there in the middle of all the downed trees. What was the purpose behind it? Why did they put it here? Why did they tear up the area like this? With everything we found, we also found more questions.

We passed the torn-up areas and continued up the mountain. I was tired as this was the furthest we had walked so far. We stopped for Paul to get a look at the map. I sat down on the ground to rest while he looked. He assumed that we had a half to three-quarters of a mile left. It didn't sound too bad when you said it. It was quite a way when you walked it. I lay back on the ground and looked up through the trees. A few white puffy clouds were dancing on a beautiful blue sky.

Spring was here, and I was ready for the warmer weather. Then I heard a whistle. It was shrill and loud, just like a man would make. I quickly sat up and looked around. I didn't see anyone. I was about to ask Paul about it when we heard a tree knock that sounded close.

To my surprise, Paul sat down on the ground beside me. "Let's just listen for a while," he said. I lay back on the ground while Paul sat beside me. We heard more tree knocks and another whistle. Then a strange bird call. This caused Paul to raise his eyebrows.

It was the strangest bird I had ever heard. Then somewhere in the forest, a hoot owl answered it back. It sounded like they were all around us. I reached into my pocket and pulled out my phone. I turned on the recorder and lay it beside me. I wished I had thought to do this earlier. I was thrilled to be able to hear the noises that we assumed were made by a Bigfoot. From what we had learned, getting to hear this much was considered rare. Finally, the forest grew silent again, and it was time for us to move on.

As we walked further and further up the mountain, I began to grow more uncomfortable. There was no apparent reason for me to feel this way. I kept telling myself that I was being silly and pushed the negative feelings to the back of my mind. I was lost in my own thoughts when Paul stopped in front of me.

Thinking he had seen something, I stopped and didn't make a sound.

"This had to be what he was talking about," Paul said.

I looked around his shoulder and was amazed at what I saw. The view was simply breathtaking, from where we stood.

The mountain opened out into a small valley clearing, where the river ran right through the middle of it.

It was beautiful. It was so pretty that it didn't even look like it belonged in these woods. The river flowed calmly through the valley, making it look like a great place to fish.

"No wonder he told us not to miss this," I exclaimed. "It's gorgeous here."

"I think we agree that we have found our camping spot," Paul stated.

"We certainly have," I responded.

Paul and I decided to gather some firewood before we headed back. It would make it easier for us tomorrow when we were getting our camp set up.

I still had the thought in the back of my head that something wasn't right. As beautiful as this place was, it just didn't feel right.

I gathered the firewood from the edge of the forest and carried arm full after arm full, piling it up at the edge of the clearing. As Paul and I worked, I noticed that the woods were unusually quiet.

I assumed that no one had been here for ages, so the local wildlife was keeping quiet and watching us along with any Bigfoot that may be in the area.

Paul and I sat down to rest before starting our long walk back. I was so tired it felt like I could have laid there on the ground and slept all night. I was just about to doze off when something growled loudly from just inside the tree line. My blood went cold. My heart began to race, and my stomach knotted up. Paul slowly stood up and reached for my hand. "Nice and slow," he said. We were both watching the tree line now but didn't see a thing. Paul and I started to walk slowly away with him, looking back every few seconds. We never saw what made that horrible noise. However, it sure let us know that it didn't want us around. Now I was wondering if our camping there was such a good idea.

For most of our walk back to the cabin, something walked with us, just out of sight to our right. When we would stop, it would stop. You could tell by the way the leaves crunched that it was something with two legs. Paul and I both kept trying to see what it was. It stayed just out of our line of sight.

I didn't feel uncomfortable or scared. But I could feel a presence other than our own.

That evening Paul and I packed up everything we would need for a few days in the woods.

Packing our gear in was always tiring. But this would be more of a walk than either one of us was used to.

On the way to our campsite, we stopped and checked the treats we had left. The second peanut butter jar was now half-full, and both lids were completely missing. We couldn't figure out what was happening. I hadn't brought any peanut butter with us today, so I left two granola bars on the stump to see what would happen. Paul said that we might need to get us a couple of trail cameras. I don't know why we didn't think of this before! Then we might have photos of what was going on! I was now excited about our next trip to town!

Both bags of apples were gone this time. Just like the last one, they have pulled off the rope they were tied to. There were no traces of the bags or the apples. Paul and I did an extensive investigation in the nearby area. We even raked back leaves to see if we could find tracings of the eaten apples. There was nothing anywhere. There were no definite answers. We could only assume that a smaller animal would have left bits and pieces behind. Something had taken both bags of apples that were roughly ten feet off the ground.

And there was no trace of them ever having been here. Neither Paul nor I could come up with a logical explanation. Could a raccoon untie the knots on the rope and run away with a whole bag of apples? I guess it might be possible, but highly unlikely.

This is exactly why we needed cameras. Then we would know for sure.

Paul didn't have apples with him today. We had only brought what we had to since our backpacks were already loaded down with camping supplies. Paul took his backpack off and set it on the ground. He unzipped the top compartment and rummaged around. I wondered what he was looking for. Finally, after a lot of searching on his part, he held up a large Honey Bun. He stuck this in the fork of the tree where the apples had been tied. "I know anything can get if from here." He said. "Let's just see what happens." We left our new treats and made our way up to our campsite.

It was well past lunchtime when we walked out into the clearing. We decided to eat a small lunch and rest a little before we set up our camp. The long walk, combined with the heavyweight of our packs, had worn us both out. It wasn't but a few minutes after we ate that Paul and I both were sound asleep under the warm sun.

When Paul woke me up, I was startled that we had both slept well over an hour. This was not like us!

We laughed and teased each other about getting old and needing a nap.

It didn't take us long to get our camp set up, and Paul went down to the river to fish. This left me alone to explore.

I walked around the edge of the woods, looking at plants. I didn't see many of the plants that I expected to. It appeared that they had been dug up, or were missing altogether. It was exactly like what I had run into back at the cabin. I had always been able to find Broadleaf Plantain, but there was none here. As I slowly walked the edge of the woods, I saw a few random arches just inside the tree line. I came across an amazingly huge X. It was so big and so obvious that it startled me when I first saw it. I wondered what it meant. It was not very welcoming, that was for sure. I saw what I thought to be a few Bigfoot prints, but they were only partial prints, so I ignored them. I walked back over to our campsite. I thought about going fishing with Paul, but instead, I pulled out my books and found a good spot just at the edge of the clearing. I kicked away the leaves, and pine needles then settled in with my back against a tree. I was going to try to familiarize myself with the plants in this area. There had to be more out there that I was missing. It wasn't long until I was utterly lost in my books.

I'm not sure how long I had been there. The sun was setting, and it was getting harder for me to read.

I looked up to see where Paul was, and that's when I saw it! It was standing just inside the tree line where Paul was fishing! Paul had his back to this creature and had no clue that it was there!

My heart leaped up in my throat. My stomach knotted up, and sweat broke out on my forehead. I was both scared to death and fascinated. I wasn't sure what I should do. Apparently, it hadn't seen me sitting over here in the trees. Luckily it didn't seem to be moving toward Paul. It seemed to be hiding behind the brush and watching him. For the few seconds that I watched this thing, it appeared to be slightly swaying back and forth, just like Brett had said. My eyes kept jumping from it to Paul. It was much closer to Paul than I was. This scared me. If it went after him, it would be on him before I could get there. What could I do? I glanced around quickly for some sort of weapon. That's when I saw my can of bear spray lying beside my boot. I grabbed it and slowly stood up. I walked toward Paul, acting like I didn't even know that this creature was standing there. I kept watching it out of the corner of my eye. It crouched down behind the brush as I approached. I could still see its fur between the leaves. I walked up beside Paul and loudly asked how the fishing was going.

I then squatted down and wrote, *don't turn around*, in the sand by the river. Paul read it and raised his eyebrows at me without saying a word. Without turning my head, I glanced back over at the bushes, and it was gone! There was nothing there! This thing had not made any sound at all, how could it be gone?

"It's gone,"! I exclaimed. Looking at the tree line.

Paul turned around then. "What did you see"? He asked.

"There was a bigfoot right there. Just inside the tree line!" I said. Pointing at where the Bigfoot had stood.

Paul lay down his fishing pole and walked over to the bushes. He was looking at the ground as he pulled back the undergrowth. "Right here,"! He said excitedly.

I hurried over to where he was. You could plainly see the indentations on the ground where this thing had stood only moments earlier.

"What was it doing"? Paul asked excitedly. "Did you get a picture"?

It had never crossed my mind to take a picture until Paul mentioned it. How stupid of me!

"I think it was watching you fish," I told him. When I looked up, I saw it standing there watching you. It was just standing there, swaying back and forth.

It hid down behind the bushes when I came over to you. And then it just disappeared". I told him.

"It never crossed my mind to get a picture," I sadly told him.

Paul and I decided to head back to our camp and get dinner started before it got dark. We fried the fish Paul had caught along with few potatoes I had brought.

The food was amazing. I always wondered why food cooked over a campfire tasted better than the food cooked at home.

The night was cool, but not cold. It was amazing to sit by the fire and listen to the gentle sound of the river. I felt like I could stay here forever.

"Have you noticed something"? Paul asked.

I did not have a clue what he was talking about. "What"? I asked.

"We are sitting out here tonight close to the river, and there are no crickets or frogs at all. Everything is completely silent".

I hadn't paid any attention to this, but he was right. Now that he had mentioned it, the silence was almost deafening. "That is strange," I said. "Maybe it's going to rain," I added. "Don't they all go silent before it rains"? Paul and I both looked up at the starry sky.

There were no clouds tonight. That couldn't be the reason. I was just about to ask Paul what he thought was causing it. When I heard something walking in the leaves behind our tent. It sounded human. Paul heard it the same time I did because he turned to look at me without speaking. We sat there and listened to the footsteps.

There was an occasional small grunt. Then the steps began to sound like two things were walking about. Paul and I continued to sit there quietly, listening. The grunts and footsteps carried on for a little while, then everything was silent again. Paul told me that he had read that sometimes the woods would grow quiet when there is a Bigfoot in the area. This both excited and scared me. I did want to see one up close. However, I didn't think I wanted to do it out here in the dark. Now I wondered if this had been a good idea. I had my doubts.

Paul got up to put more kindling on the fire. We would stoke it one more time and watch it die down before going to bed. This is what we usually did when camping.

As Paul was putting the sticks on the fire, something landed at his foot with a thump. I couldn't see what it was from where I was sitting.

I watched as he bent down and picked something up. A rock! And not just a small pebble. This rock was easily the size of his palm. I was shocked! Paul was smiling like a little boy that had just found a treasure. He came back over and sat down beside me, holding the rock out for me to see. It was a river rock. Of course, it was dry now, but by the smoothness, you could tell that it had once been in the water.

I decided to keep it. After all, how many people can say that they have a rock that was thrown by a Bigfoot? I knew I would never tell anyone this, but I still wanted to keep it.

The fire was beginning to die down, and it was casting strange shadows into the surrounding trees. It was causing me to see shadows that I thought were moving. I kept reassuring myself that nothing was there.

Paul and I crawled into our small tent and made ourselves comfortable. The night was eerily silent.

It wasn't long before I heard Paul snoring. I think this was the loudest thing in the forest! I turned over a few times, trying to get comfortable so I could fall asleep. I couldn't understand this.

I was usually asleep before Paul. Maybe it was the fact that we were in Bigfoot territory that was messing with my subconscious. I lay there thinking about this when I heard what I thought to be a small rock hit the side of the tent. My blood went cold. Not now.

Please don't let them start doing this now. I'm not sure why I felt this way. I guess I felt more vulnerable inside the tent, where I couldn't see what was around me.

The second rock hit, and then a third. They sounded to be small. Should I wake Paul or let him sleep. The next two rocks seemed to be a little bigger. I had sat up in my sleeping bag, and the adrenaline was kicking in. I was straining my ears to see if I could tell which direction the rocks were coming from. That's when I heard it. The footsteps were back. Something was walking toward the tent. It sounded like it was already close, yet it was still coming in our direction. Now I was really getting scared.

"Paul," I whispered loudly. He grunted but didn't answer me. "Paul, wake up," I whispered a little louder.

"What is it"? He sleepily asked.

"Something is coming toward the tent," I told him.

Paul turned over in his sleeping bag.


"What did you hear"? He whispered.

"I heard rocks hit the tent, but now there is some walking too," I whispered back.

Paul sat up now. We both listened to the silence. I was about to give up thinking the footsteps had stopped when they started back, closer this time.

They stopped right outside the tent! I quickly reached over and grabbed Paul's arm. Something was standing right at the back of our tent! Paul reached out and picked up his pistol unsnapping the holster. That one single snap sounded excessively loud. I held my breath and listened for a reaction to the noise. There was nothing. Nothing at all. Paul leaned over even further and grabbed his can of bear spray. Why hadn't I thought of this? I immediately began feeling around my own sleeping bag for my can. We always kept them within reach while sleeping. I found it! My hand grasped the cold metal with my finger finding the trigger. I immediately felt better.

It felt like we sat there forever, listening.

"Let's try to get some sleep," Paul whispered.

After not hearing anything for a while, I was ready to agree with him.


Paul and I settled into our sleeping bags once more.

Just as I closed my eyes, a scream came from the river that caused me to sit straight up and clasp my hand over my mouth. It was loud! Before Paul or I could say a word, a second scream came from behind the tent. This scream sounded like it was only a few feet away. It was so loud that it vibrated through my chest, and I swear I felt the vibrations on my butt through the ground that the tent was sitting on.

I have never experienced anything so loud. It hurt my ears instantly and sent a shot of raw adrenaline straight through my whole body. I would have been up on my feet had the tent allowed.

Paul grabbed his gun and quickly unzipped the tent. I felt vulnerable inside the tent, but I was even more scared once Paul unzipped it. He shined his flashlight straight toward the river. It lit up the whole area in a single flash. I didn't move from my spot. I didn't want to see it standing out there. Paul was on his hands and knees, shinning the light all around the front side of the tent. Finally, he turned out the light and zipped the canvas back. "I can't see a thing," he stated. I felt a little better with the tent zipped. But I wasn't sure what scared me the most. The fact that they were out there or the fact that they were out there and we couldn't see them.

After a while of not hearing anything else, Paul lay back down in his sleeping bag. How could he go to sleep?

I was wide-awake with large amounts of adrenaline surging through my body. What if they come back?

What if they were angry that we were here? Were they just curious?

I was still sitting in the same spot pondering these and many other questions when the sun topped the mountain.

After breakfast, Paul and I went to look around for any evidence. We found some broken branches and a few places where the leaves seemed to be packed down as if something had stood there. But we didn't find anything significant.

Paul decided that we would leave our tent, but head back to the cabin for a day or two. I was exhausted, and Paul wanted to do some more research. This sounded great to me. I wanted a shower and sleep. I wondered if I would be up to the long walk back.

We left the majority of our things and only carried the food with us. There was no sense in leaving it there for the wild animals to carry off. We didn't check our treats on the way out. I was just too tired to care.

We finally made it to the cabin around three. It would have been earlier if I hadn't had to stop and rest so much.

We both grabbed showers, and Paul headed down to the library while I slept on the couch.

I chose to sleep downstairs in case anything happened, I would hear it. Usually, I wouldn't have stayed in the cabin alone. But today I was so tired that I actually didn't care. I would be asleep within minutes anyway. I listened to our car drive away, and the next thing I remembered was Paul turning on lights waking me up. It was eight already!

Paul sat some brown paper bags on the bar and went to make coffee. I headed to the bathroom before checking out the bags. I could smell the burgers, and my mouth was already watering.

Over a dinner of amazing burgers and fries, Paul told me what he had found during his research. Most of the local sightings had been on the BLM land adjacent to Brett's. That made sense because Brett's is posted as Private property. Even if someone had seen something here, they couldn't report it without getting into trouble. Paul had also gone back to the same diner, hoping to run into the man that had marked our map. Unfortunately, he wasn't there this time.

I began cleaning up the remains of our dinner when Paul got up and walked out of the kitchen door. I wondered what he was doing. He came back in a few minutes later with more bags. After placing them on the counter, he pulled a rather large box from the first bag. It was a camouflage trail camera! He had purchased three cameras and three digital recorders with headphones!

The next morning, I was excited to get our things back up to the campsite. In my excitement, I didn't stop to consider the fact that this was adding weight to the things we would eventually have to bring back down.

I poured myself a cup of coffee and walked out onto the back porch. I couldn't believe what I was seeing!

It made me extremely happy and scared to death at the same time. Right in the middle of the porch rail sat a red apple! It had not been here yesterday, so something or someone had to have brought it last night. Why? What did this mean? There were hundreds of questions again.

Paul was as excited as I was to see the apple. He quickly went to check for prints, but there was nothing there.

We packed up our new gear and headed out right after coffee.

This time, we stopped to check the treats we had left because Paul wanted to set up a trail camera and audio.

The peanut butter jars were now on the ground by the stump. They were completely empty except for a small amount at the bottom. The two lids lay on top of the stump. This was strange because the one had been missing the last time we checked. My granola bars were gone, but the wrappers were lying on the ground. Paul picked up one and examined it carefully. He was pleased when he showed me that there were no teeth marks on it at all. So how did an animal get it open? In all honesty, it looked like Paul or I would have opened it. It was pulled apart at the top and then torn down the seam. The second one was the same way. After I took pictures of everything, Paul sat the audio recorder in a waterproof bag and placed it in a nearby tree.

He placed some leaves and branches with it. When He finished, I was shocked. I couldn't even tell that it was there and I had watched him do it!

We moved on to the apples, and the Honey Bun Paul had left. The Honey Bun wrapper was on the ground by the tree. It looked just like the Granola wrappers. It had no bite marks on it. I couldn't explain this. Any animal would have chewed through the wrapper to get to the food inside.

Paul set up a trail camera facing the tree where he had left the apples. This time, we had a couple of yellow apples, a Honey Bun, and a pack of cheese crackers. We arranged the treats in the fork of the tree and put a few on limbs. Paul made sure that they were secure where no wind could blow them down. I was excited to see what our camera would reveal. The excitement carried me right on to our camp. I think I half expected our tent to be down our torn up when we arrived. But everything was just as we had left it.

The first thing we did was find places for the other two trail cameras and the audio. We wanted the cameras to be facing our tent from the front and the back—the audio we just placed randomly inside the tree line. I was so excited to see what we would capture overnight.

Paul decided to try to catch some fish before dark. So I positioned myself again just at the tree line.

I wanted to be able to see if anything walked out. I made myself comfortable and began to read the notes Paul had taken the day before. I was shocked at how much information he had found in such a short time. Some of it we already knew, but there were other things I had never heard of. Some people claim to see lights in the sky or forest just before a sighting. And there are some that claim Bigfoot is not flesh and blood.

They think it is some sort of interdimensional being. (An entity capable of traveling through unusual dimensional rifts that few other entities can enter.) Wow. I had never even considered anything like this. What caused these people to think this way? I wasn't very close, but what I had seen looked to be flesh and blood. And what about the howls and screams? How could anything not flesh and blood make such a noise? This was becoming more than I could wrap my brain around. I had assumed it was some sort of ape. Then over millions of years, it evolved into the Bigfoot of today.

It observed man on almost a daily basis. So why wouldn't it utilize the concepts of man? Just then, I heard a tree knock off to my left. It sounded distant. I strained my ears to listen for another. Hearing this knock brought on even more questions? How do they make this knocking sound? Do they hit a tree with a stick as men do? Do they slap a tree with their bare hand?

Is it a sound that they can make with their mouths? And why do they build tree structures? I cannot think of any purpose they would have. Most of them are too small for the Bigfoot to actually use. Is this a way that they communicate with one another? There had been many others before me with these same questions.

Some had even taken them to the grave. Would I ever know what this was all about, or would our very best attempts be just as futile?

I watched as Paul stood up with a stringer of fish. He looked at me proudly, holding them up as if they were a trophy. I waved to him and stood up. Just then, I heard another knock. I felt like they were either watching us. Or letting each other know that we were back. A small smile ran across my lips. I knew that with every little interaction, we were one step closer to solving this age-old puzzle.

After another dinner of fish and fried potatoes, Paul and I sat listening to the gentle sound of the river.

From where we had positioned our tent, it was far back enough that we got the trickling water sound with blurps and gurgles. Just enough to be soothing. The fire was popping and crackling, sending the occasional sparks storm into the sky. I was more relaxed than I had been in a long time. Tonight we were serenaded with frogs and crickets. I think hearing them helped me to relax.

I was yawning well before the fire had died down. Paul walked down to the river and brought back a pan of water to put the fire out. We crawled into our tent, and I was quickly asleep.

The next morning I woke before Paul. I decided to get the coffee started and have it ready when he woke up.

I stepped out of the tent into the chilly morning. The sun wasn't up enough to chase away the fog and the nights chill. A scream caught in my throat! I just stood there in disbelief with my hand over my mouth. Not even ten feet in front of me was the biggest X I had ever seen! It was made by using two trees that were roughly ten feet tall and twenty-five inches in circumference! This thing was massive!

"Paul," my voice squeaked.

"Paul," I said a little louder, with my voice cracking.

"Paul,"! I yelled. Not actually meaning it to come out as a yell. Paul came scrambling out of the tent beside me.

"What"? "Are you OK"? "HOLY COW"

Paul slowly walked toward the X. "This is magnificent," he exclaimed.

I did not like the thought of these creatures doing this while we were sleeping. I was having a moment of sheer panic.

Paul must have realized this when he looked at me. He paused for a moment and then said. "Come here, Candi. You've got to see this."

I slowly walked the few feet over to Paul. I was all of a sudden freezing to the point of my teeth chattering.

Paul put his arm around me and began to point out specific things about the structure. Things that proved it wasn't man-made. I already knew it wasn't, and it set my nerves on edge.

Paul could sense my unease, so he pulled the trees down and drug them over to our woodpile. He put the coffee on and sent me into the tent to find a sweater.

I slipped my sweater on and climbed back out of the tent. I had many things to think about. Did I really want to continue pursuing these creatures? Or was I ready to just walk away and forget about all of it? It was going to have to be one way or the other.

Just then, Paul sat his cup down and went to the back of the tent. I had assumed to relieve himself until he came back carrying one of our cameras. My heart skipped a beat. Had we caught it on camera? Did we have images? I was immediately excited. I had just answered my own question. I was scared. But I wasn't quite ready to walk away.

Paul brought the camera over and sat down beside me. He rewound the video so we could watch from the beginning. Nothing at all happened until just after dark.

The light from our fire cast strange shadows on the backside of the tent. You could hear our snores and sounds of things being moved around. But the video only captured the back of the tent.

Paul walked over to get the next camera from the tree line. I was sure this one had caught something. It had been facing the front of our tent all night. It had to have caught them creating the X. Once again, Paul rewound the video. We watched ourselves until Paul put the fire out, and we crawled into the tent. A short time later, we heard what sounded like footsteps approached the camera from behind, and then it was tilted down. It was now recording the ground in front of the camera. Our tent could no longer be seen. How did this happen? I could only assume that this was done by one of the Bigfoot. But we had no proof. We could still hear audio of things moving around. But without video, we had no proof. Did they know this? Were they that smart? It sure appeared that way.

Paul and I were both disappointed that we didn't capture anything. But we still had the third camera that we would grab on the way back to the cabin. Maybe, with it being out there by itself, it would catch something.

Paul went and checked on the audio recorders. They were both still recording. He decided to turn them off until evening.

Being so disappointed in the cameras, neither of us was interested in listening to the audio. We decided to cook some breakfast and then go for a hike.

Paul and I hiked to the top of the mountain closest to us. The view from the top was amazing. We didn't see as many structures as we had down in the valley. But there was still evidence that something had been through this area as well. There were a few small structures and a few arches. What puzzled me the most was the number of river rocks up here. It seemed like every few feet, there was a smooth river rock laying on top of the leaves and pine needles. I had picked up three and dropped them in my backpack.

Paul advised me that I wouldn't want to keep doing that. It hadn't occurred to me that I would be carrying a backpack filled with rocks back to the cabin in a few days. I guess I should be more selective in the ones I picked up.

We enjoyed our hike and made it back to the camp in time to fish for dinner. Paul and I struck up a friendly competition on the fishing. He even told me that he would give me a head start while he sat up the cameras and turned on the audio.

By the time he finished and made it back to the river, I had already caught four trout! This was a record for me.

Paul was the fisherman in our family. He teased me about it being, "beginners luck." Paul caught two more fish for us and began cleaning them while I went to get our fire started.

I grabbed some limbs off of our pile and dragged them down to the fire pit. I didn't notice it until I had gone back over to the woodpile a few times, but the trees that Paul had placed there this morning was gone! I looked around the area but saw no sign of them. How do trees just disappear? I grabbed up a few more sticks and went back to the fire. I would tell Paul about it when he got over here. Maybe he had drug them somewhere else.

Paul was as shocked as I was to find the trees gone. He walked into the woods to see if there was any sign of them being moved. He didn't find anything, not even any drag marks on the ground. It appeared that whatever had taken the trees had lifted them up and carried them away. No man could have done this. Paul was only able to pull them along the ground. Now I wished we had left the cameras running while we were gone today.

After dinner that night, Paul stoked up our fire and pulled out a pack of playing cards. We played a few hands and then just enjoyed letting the fire die out.

The night was once again silent. There was something close by.

Knowing this didn't scare me as bad as it had in the beginning. They didn't seem to be aggressive towards us at all. I guess they were just curious. That night, I was completely relaxed when Paul and I crawled into the tent. I knew they weren't going to do anything to harm us.

A few times during the night, I heard what I thought to be footsteps on the leaves and a few soft grunts. I quickly fell back asleep each time. I know longer feared anything harming us. We had been here so long that if they wanted us gone, they would have scared us away by now.

The next two days went by pretty much the same. We hiked and fished during the day, and the nights were eerily silent.

We didn't catch anything on our cameras for one reason or another. I was starting to feel like they were a big waste of money.

Our last day camping dawned overcast and threatening to rain. Paul and I contemplated heading back to the cabin. But we decided to tough it out one more day before we headed back. We had decided that we would go home and come back in the fall and see if things had changed. So this would be our last chance to camp before leaving. I had packed our rain gear so if it got to bad we could just pack up and walk back in the rain.

We spent most of the day hiking as we had done before. There were a few times that we heard the footsteps walking along with us. It was staying just to the right of us past some thick underbrush. We couldn't see a thing, but the sound of the steps let us know that it was with us. Sometimes the steps would fade away as if it had walked in another direction, but they always caught back up to us. I was beginning to feel like we had an unseen friend enjoying our walk.

We stopped for a break and dug some snacks out of our backpacks. We hadn't been sitting but a minute when the small rocks started coming from the underbrush. It was almost like some kid was hiding in the bushes playing.

Paul tossed a few rocks in the direction they were coming from, and the same stone would be thrown back. This went on for a little while and then completely stopped. The woods had grown quiet. In all honesty, I don't know when they went quiet, but that was when I noticed it. When we left our campsite this morning, the birds had been singing.

After our break, Paul thought that we should head back.

The clouds were growing darker, and he wanted to get in a little fishing before it started to rain. This time, the footsteps didn't follow us.

There was a fine mist falling when we made it back to camp. We were shocked to see that our food, which Paul always ties up in a tree, had been pulled down and gone through! I quickly looked around our camp and the surrounding area. This was plainly the work of a black bear. Paul and I walked the tree line together just to make sure that it wasn't still close by. We didn't even see any signs of the bear. But we were confident that it had been in our camp.

Since the threat of the bear was gone. Paul went fishing, and I began to pack up our gear. I knew we wouldn't leave until morning. But I wanted to keep everything as dry as I possibly could. Once it all got wet, it would be much heavier.

Paul managed to get the fish cleaned and cooked before the rain set in. We had our last meal huddled inside our small tent. I have to admit that it was a bit cozy, and I loved the sound of the rain falling on the tarp above us.

Paul and I used a flashlight to play a few hands of cards before going to sleep. The battery on the flashlight was beginning to flicker, so we turned it off and crawled into our sleeping bags.

I'm not sure how long I had been asleep when I heard a small rock hit the back of the tent. I lay there and listened to them a while. I fell back asleep because the next thing I heard was Paul.

"Candi. Wake up and get your boots on". I wasn't sure what was going on. I was still half asleep when something grabbed the back of the tent and shook it really hard! A scream like a woman was being murdered came from the river! My heart flew up in my throat! Paul was helping me get my right boot on with the aid of the flickering flashlight. Just as I got my left boot on, the tent collapsed on us!. Paul kept muttering reassuring words as he tried to unzip the now flattened tent.

"It's going to be OK." "We know the way back." "We're going to be fine."

I heard the zipper and heard paul struggling with the tent flap. The flashlight went out just as the first bolt of lightning flashed across the sky, followed by the deep rumble of thunder. In the sudden bright light, I could now see all of our stuff that we were climbing over to get out. Paul stopped halfway out of the tent. "Grab my gun, Candi." He said.

I frantically fumbled for the gun. I grabbed the bear spray and threw it out of my way.

I wished I had thought to give it to Paul too. But I was only focused on the gun.

I found it after a couple of minutes and thrust it into his outstretched hand. Paul climbed out of the tent with me on his heels.

The lightning lit up the whole valley floor. We got to our feet in the pouring rain. It looked as if shadows moved just inside the tree line.

The scream came again. This time it was just inside the trees to our left. Paul spun around, slapping the flashlight on his palm. Now the scream came from behind us. Paul turned again just as the flashlight came on. These screams went on back and forth a few times. I was terrified! I had never been so frightened in all of my life. Behind the tent, we heard a tree crashing to the ground just as one of those god awful howls roared through the valley! I could not believe what was happening. This had to be a dream. I would wake up in a minute, warm and safe in our bed with Paul beside me.

The rock came from behind us, hitting Paul in the middle of the back, knocking him off his feet. I heard him grunt, and then he went down on his hands and knees. I rushed over and tried to pull him to his feet when I got hit in the side of the head.

This time the rocks were bigger, and they weren't playing with them. I couldn't tell if it was rainwater of blood running down my face as I pulled Paul to his feet.

The rocks just kept coming! They were hitting us in the head on our backs and arms. Everywhere they connected felt like they could break a bone. These things were being thrown with tremendous force!

Paul grabbed my arm, "To the trees"! He yelled over the thunder. We could see the valley floor each time the lightning lit up the night. We ran for the trees closest to us! From the flashes of lightning, we could tell what direction we were running in. It was toward the path that would lead us back to the cabin. Getting to the cabin was our only hope now. The lightning flashed to late for us to see the downed tree. We both crashed into it, falling hard. I felt the limbs stabbing me in my neck, chest, and arms. My only thought was God, please don't let me be impaled. I scrambled to my feet as the thunder vibrated the ground. Paul was slowly getting up. I reached and grabbed his upper arm, trying to get him on his feet. The rocks were still connecting with our backs and heads.

"Come on, Paul," I screamed, "Get up"! My vision blurred as a rock hit me in the back of my head. They were trying to kill us. I knew, without any doubt.

These unseen creatures had every intention of killing us! But why? What had we done?

The rocks let up as we broke the tree line.

They were still being thrown, but most of them were hitting the trees now instead of us. The screams had started again. They were coming from all directions! Paul and I moved as fast as we could through the trees, but for some reason, I was moving more quickly than Paul. Finally, I grabbed a tree and stopped to catch my breath. Paul caught up to me.

" I want you to keep going, Candi," He said, gasping for breath. "Keep going till you get to the cabin."

"No,"! I shook my head wildly. "We're going together"! This was more than I could take. The tears ran down my face. My teeth began to chatter, and I was completely losing control.

" Candi"! Paul yelled. "Listen to me,"! "I have hurt myself, and I can't keep up, I will be behind you. I'll just be moving slower." "Now go,"! He screamed at me.

I kept my feet firmly planted. Over the sound of the storm, I could hear something coming toward us! It sounded like a train coming full force through the trees. Breaking trees and branches as it came.

Paul shoved me hard. If I hadn't been holding onto the tree, I would have probably gone down.

"GO CANDI"! He screamed at me.

I grabbed his arm and threw it over my shoulder. I wrapped my arm around his waist, and we began to run together. This was when I noticed that Paul had hurt his leg. He was having a hard time running on it, and I knew that I wouldn't be able to carry his weight all the way back to the cabin. Dear God, help us!

We were hitting trees and branches as we ran blindly through the woods. Each time the lightning flashed, I could see a little further ahead of us. That was the only way I was going to keep us from running right off of a mountain ridge. I was praying for the lightening and terrified of it at the same time. Each bolt lit up the woods, but each time it did, I wondered if we were going to be hit.

We had been running for so long that I didn't feel like I could put one foot in front of the other. I was slowing down and cursing myself for it. I had to get Paul back to the cabin!

The lightning flashed, and I saw some thick underbrush just to our left. I headed in that direction as fast as I could. Paul knew exactly what to do when we reached it.

We both dropped to our knees and crawled in. There was a big tree right in the center. I prayed the lightning wouldn't find it. Paul and I tried to control our breathing as we hid in the brush.

My heart fell, and my blood went cold as the scream vibrated the night. In the flash of lightning, I saw Paul point his gun in that direction, and he fired off four rounds. The next scream sounded different. It was painfully loud. As if one of Paul's shots had found the target.

"Let's go,"! He said, grabbing me by the arm.

We crawled out of our hiding place with dead briars and branches, finding our exposed skin. We were on our feet and running again.

We ran until my body had to stop. I grabbed the nearest tree and leaned into it. I felt like my legs couldn't hold me up anymore, and I went down hard. I was on my butt before I could think. Paul grabbed the tree next to me, breathing hard.

The lightening was getting further away now, and the thunder was distant. The storm was moving off. All I could hear was mine and Paul's raspy breathing.

This time, Paul grabbed me under the arm. "We have to keep going," he said.

We began a fast walk supporting each other the best we could. I don't know how much further we got, but this time Paul stopped.

" I can't go any further." He said. My heart sank. We had to get to the cabin. We weren't safe out here.

Paul sat down by a tree. I sat down beside him as the rain continued to fall. I pulled my legs up to my chest and wrapped my arms around them. My teeth were chattering again. Paul reached over and put his arm around my trembling body. We sat there until the sun began to come up. I was numb. I was numb from the cold and mentally numb as well, I wasn't thinking about anything. I was just existing now. I felt like I was in a horror movie. The sun was coming up. The night was over, and we were alive.

In the quiet morning, I heard a noise that I had never heard before. It was almost like a screech. I looked in that direction. Through the morning fog, I saw that there was something up in the trees. It was too large to be a bird. It moved gracefully from limb to limb. It would stop to look at us, let out a yell and then move again. My mind wasn't working. I wasn't thinking about what this thing was. I was merely watching it.

Paul slowly got to his feet. "We gotta go, Candi," he said. "That might be a baby."

Leaning on each other, we made our way down the mountain. We were walking into the cabin as the sun topped the mountains.

After checking our injuries and noting that they were all minor for the most part, Paul and I each got a shower and began to pack our things. We were on the road home by lunchtime. We didn't stop until we pulled into our own driveway.

We decided to leave our things in the woods. Even though we were both curious about the cameras, we knew that we wouldn't be going back up there to get them.

Maybe we would come back in the fall. Or perhaps we would forget that place and never look back. That was all too much to think about right now. We just wanted to be home.

Once we got home and settled back into our routine. The week at the cabin seemed more like a dream than something that actually happened. I still had a scar on my temple to let me know that it was genuine.

Paul still walked with a slight limp. But seemed to be fine other than that. I have been trying to get him to see a Doctor for some X-rays. But he's too stubborn for that.

Brett has made us an offer on the cabin. Paul and I agreed that we would make a decision on that later. We didn't tell Brett exactly what happened that week.

But we did tell him that we experienced his Bigfoot first hand.

When I look back on everything that happened, it seems more like someone's nightmare than something real.

I wouldn't believe it if someone told me. That is why Paul and I chose to keep this to ourselves.

Many questions came from our time with the Bigfoot. Questions that may never be answered in my lifetime. I'm ok with that. I have to be.

Now when Paul and I decide to go camping and hiking, we will pay more attention to our surroundings and make sure that we can get help if it's needed.

I toy with the idea of buying Brett's property if nothing else but to have it for a research area. It's going to take some time before Paul, and I can make that decision. Maybe in the fall.

Thank you for reading our story. Now you see why I decided to have our story told this way rather than talk about it to others. Paul and I are two ordinary people just like you. We just experienced something that few people have. Or should I say, "that few people ever talk about."

If you enjoyed this book, please consider leaving a review.

Also, you might want to check out some of Melissa's other titles.

1. Bigfoot Chronicles, A true story

2. Bigfoot Chronicles 2, A true story

3. Sasquatch, The Native Truth. A true story

4. Sasquatch, The Native Truth. Kecleh-Kudleh Mountain A true story

5. Sasquatch, The Native Truth. Ravens Return A true story

6. The True Haunting of a Paranormal Investigator

7. Dog Man, A True Encounter

8. Black-Eyed Kids. My Three Months of Hell. A true story

9. Family Ties. Fiction

10. Female Bigfoot Encounters. True Stories

11. Our Paranormal Reality, A True Haunting. Book 1 The Early Years

12. Our Paranormal Reality, A True Haunting. Book 2 The Investigation

13. Bigfoot, A New Reality. A True Story

14. The Birth of a Psychic with Telekinesis. A True Story

15. Lifting the Veil on All Things Paranormal, True Stories

16. Desolate Mountain, One woman's true story of survival.

17. The Watcher, A true story.

18. Bigfoot Found me. One man's true encounter with Bigfoot.

19. Goodbye. A true story of an Ouija board experience

20. Sasquatch Travels. Based on a true story.

21 Dream House

22. Breast Cancer, Faith, God & Home Free

23. Wood Bugger. One boy's true story of growing up with Bigfoot

24. The Doll.

Melissa's books can be found online at

Amazon

Barnes and Noble

Books a Million

Wal-Mart

and your local

bookstore.

Follow Melissa on,

Her Blog;
http://www.melissageorge.net/

Facebook;
https://www.facebook.com/MelissaGeorgeParanormalAuthor/

Twitter;
https://twitter.com/AuthorMelissaG

Pinterest;
https://www.pinterest.com/melissa6144/

Instagram;
https://www.instagram.com/authormelissageorge/

Get sneak peeks on upcoming books. And enjoy book giveaways with every new release!

http://melissageorge.net/

About the Author.

Melissa was born and raised in a small town in upstate South Carolina. She first became a well-known Blogger and later decided to take her writing a step further. Her first book, My Paranormal Life, A True Haunting, started out as her own private journal of her family dealing with a dark entity. But it doesn't stop there, Melissa took it even further and let her experiences help her to co-found a paranormal team and a cryptid team. She enjoys being able to reach out and help others. She has made many new friends in both of these fields, which has also led her to help others to have their story told. Melissa realizes first hand that these people have a very passionate and unique story that needs to be told. In getting these compelling stories out to the public, she hopes it will help further research in both of these fields, and just maybe the individual that shares their story with her may find some closure to their own personal nightmare. Melissa feels honored to be able to bring you true stories of the unexplained.

If you have a story you would like to see published or just want someone to talk to. I promise you complete anonymity. Melissageorge143@gmail.com

Printed in Great Britain
by Amazon

31537593R00074